AMERICAN TRADITIONAL TATTOOS

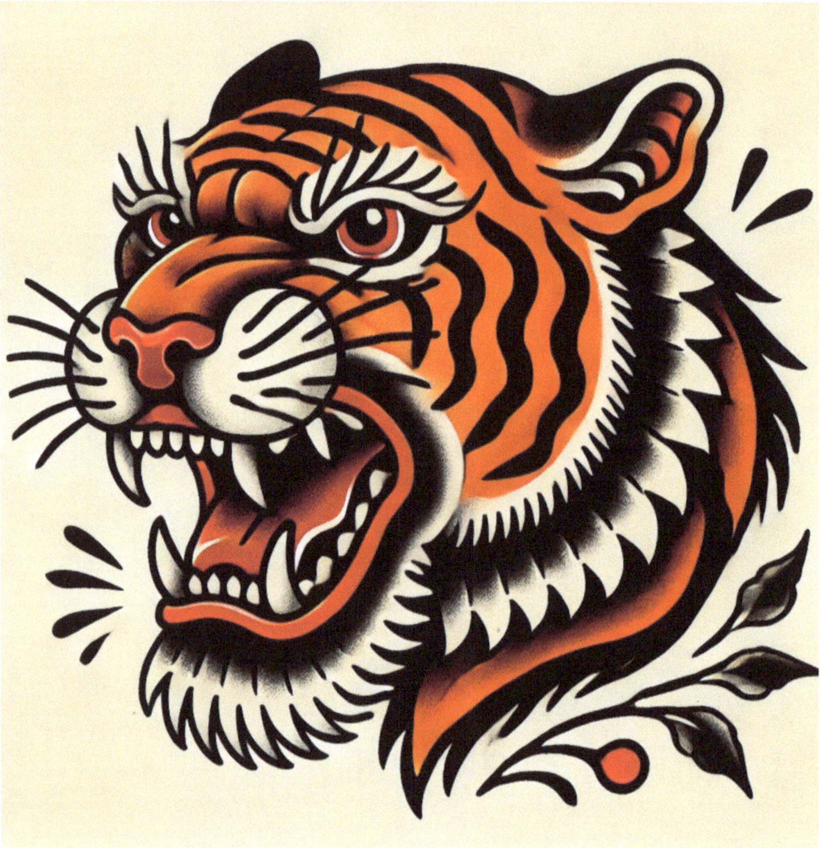

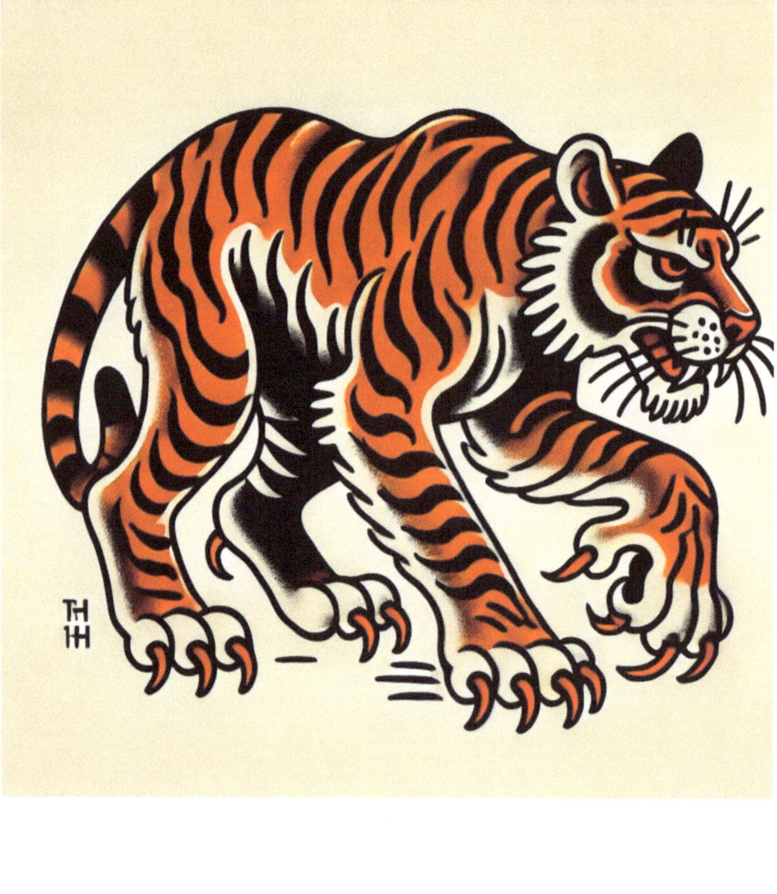

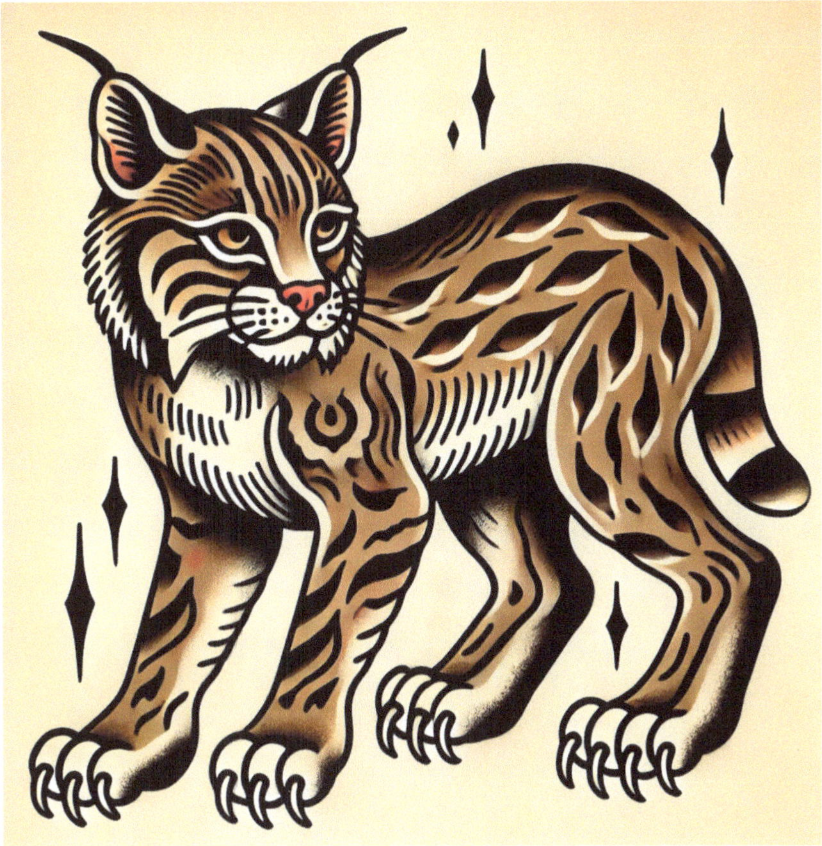

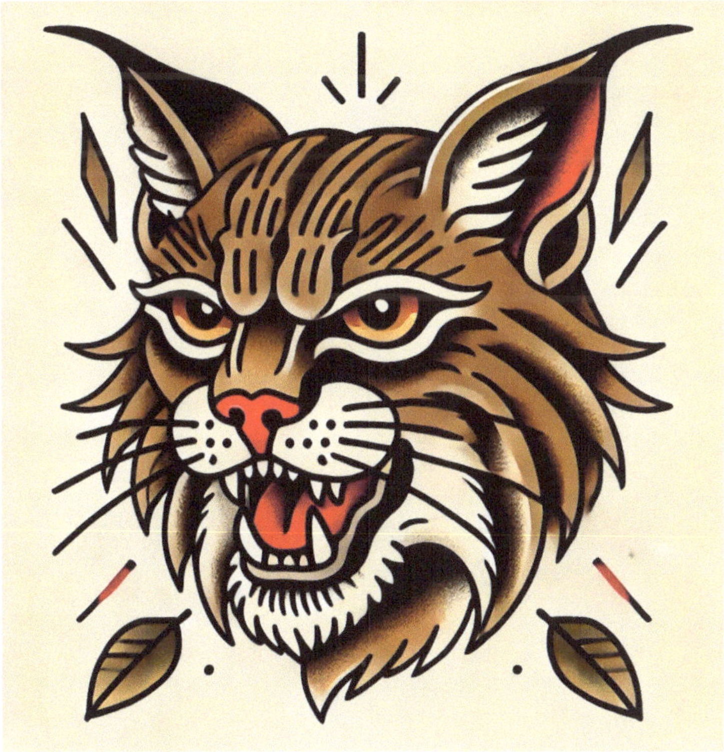

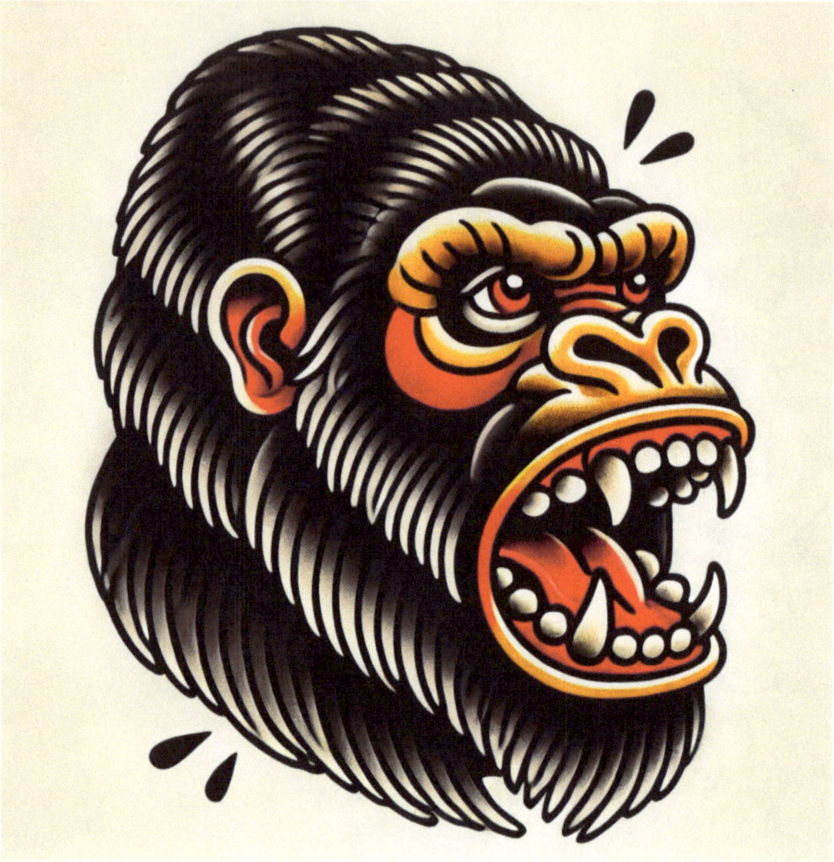

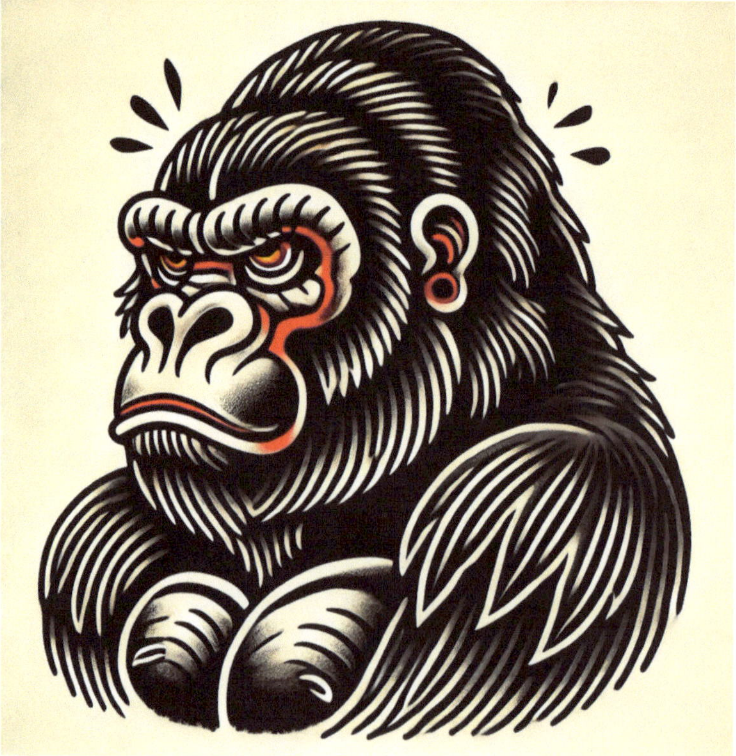

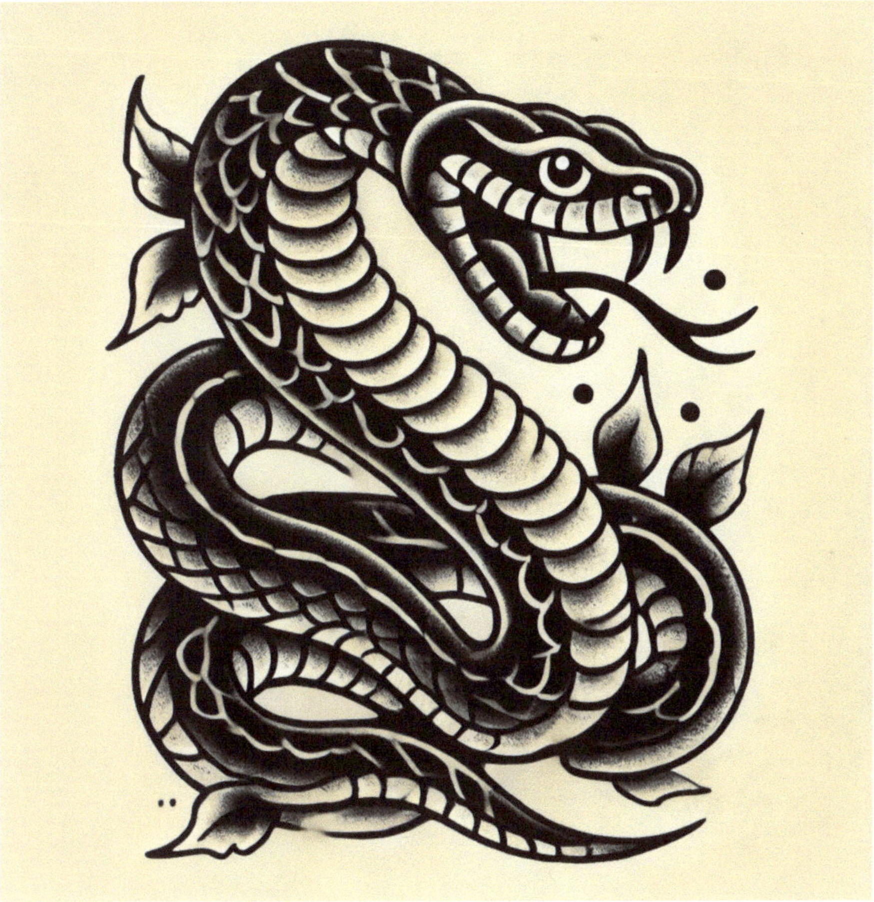
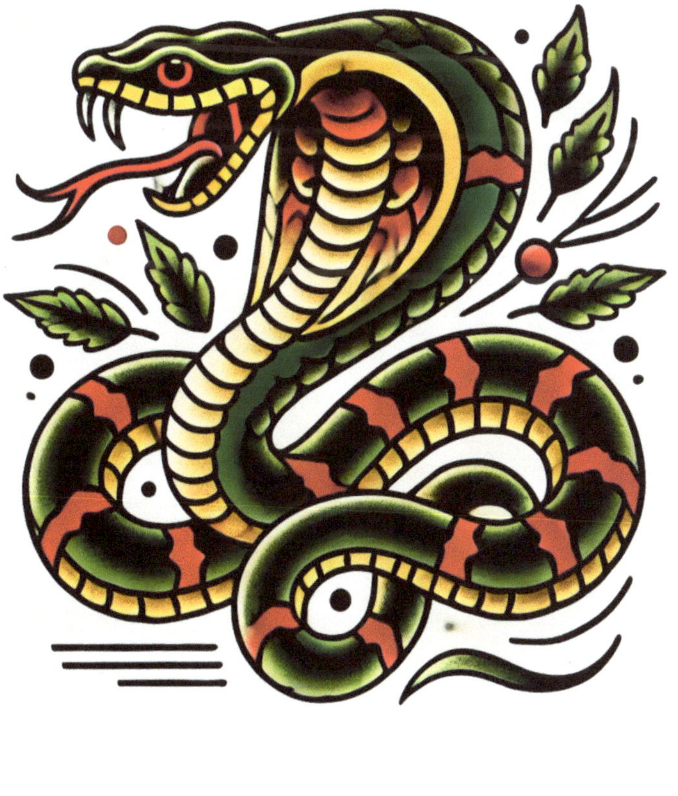

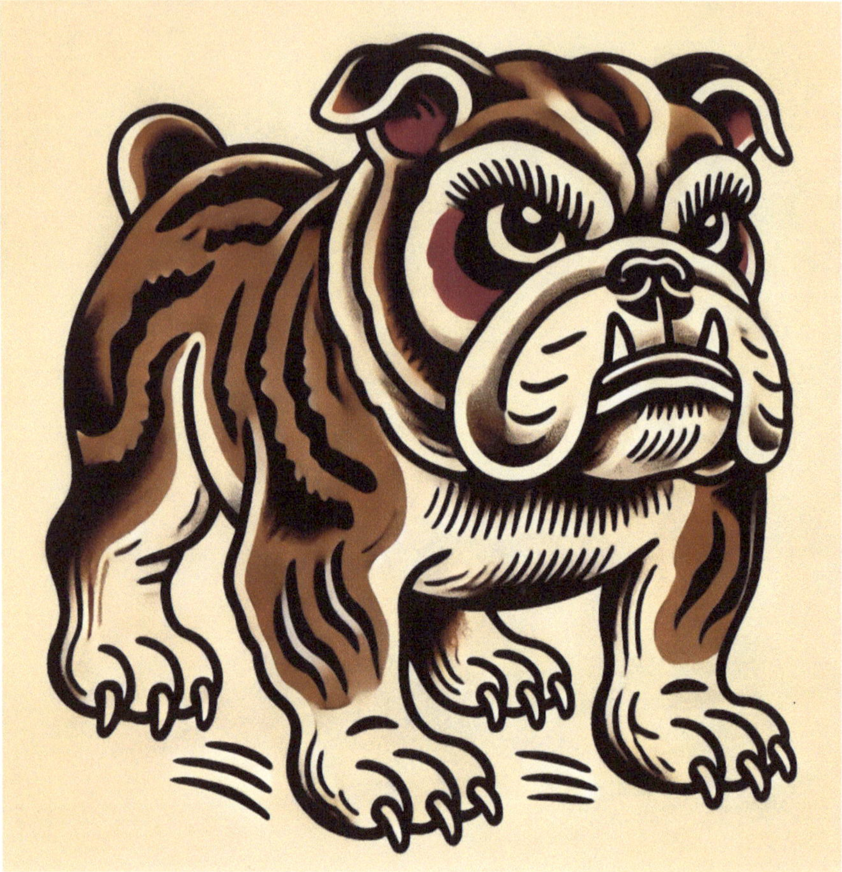

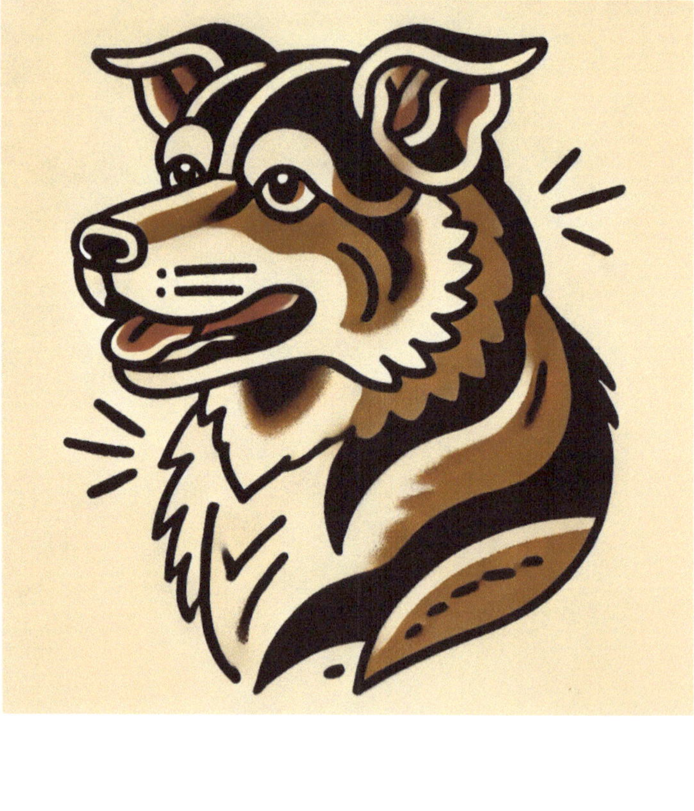

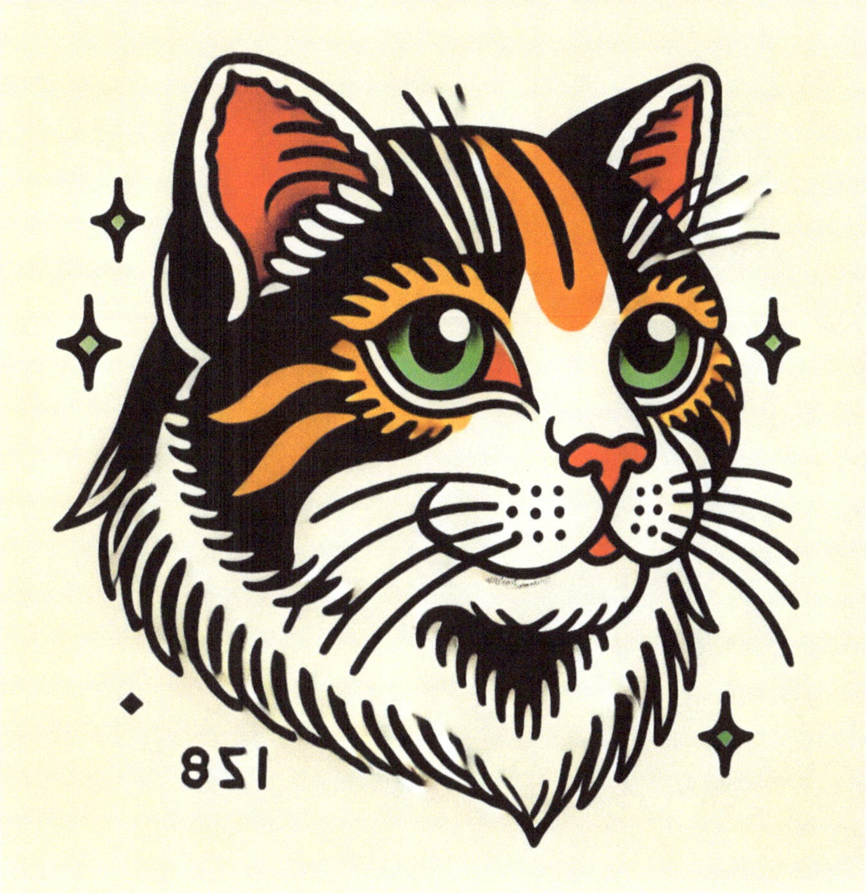

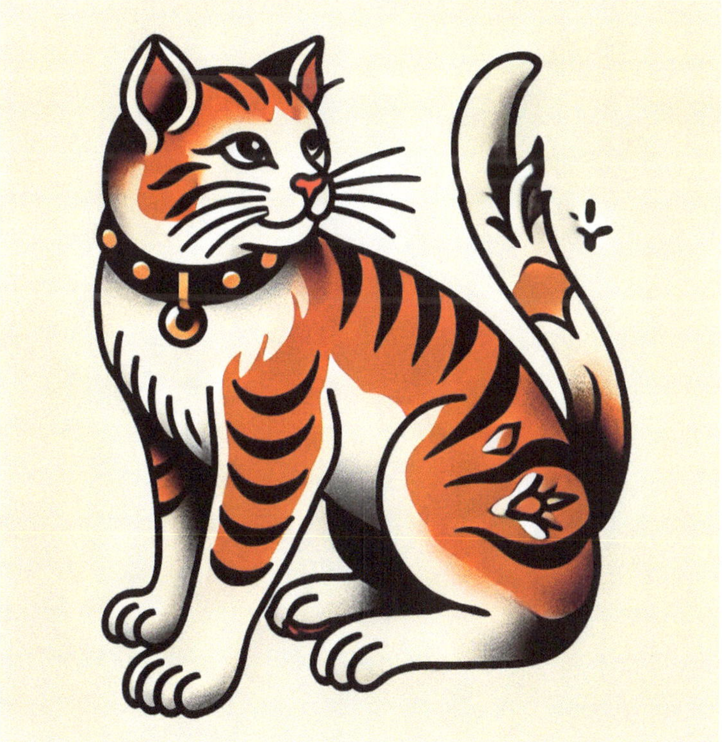

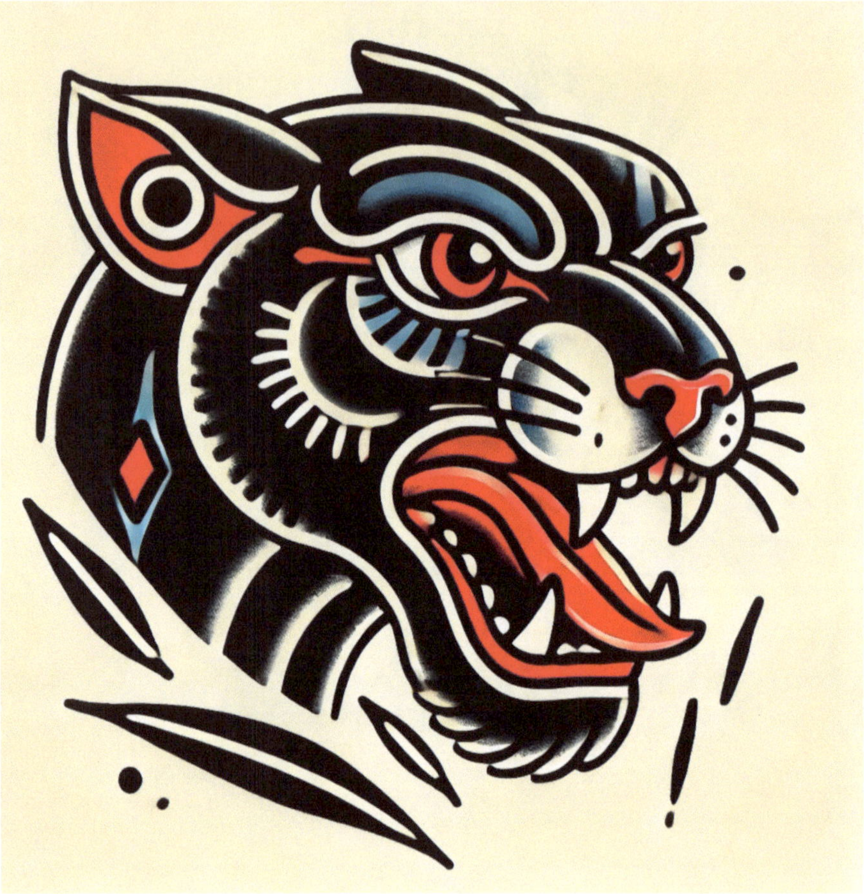

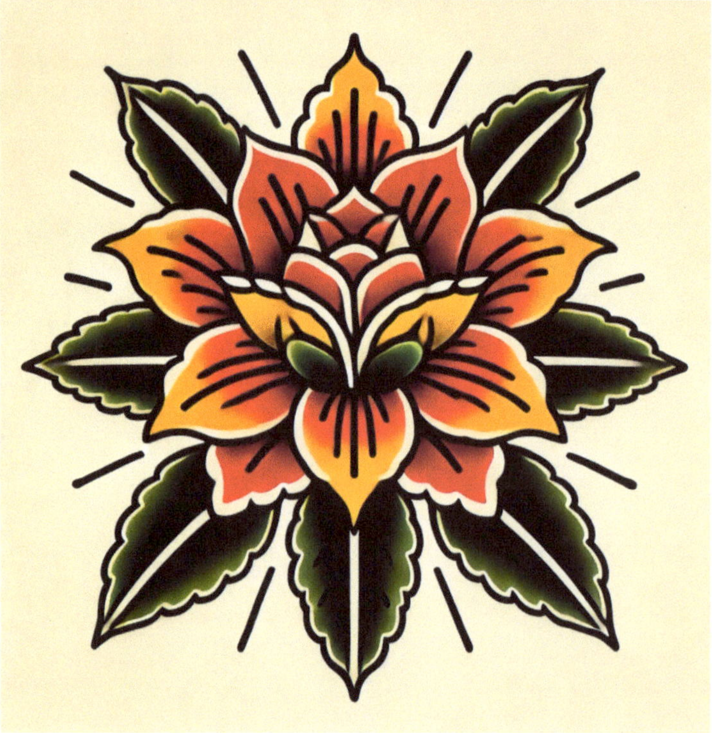

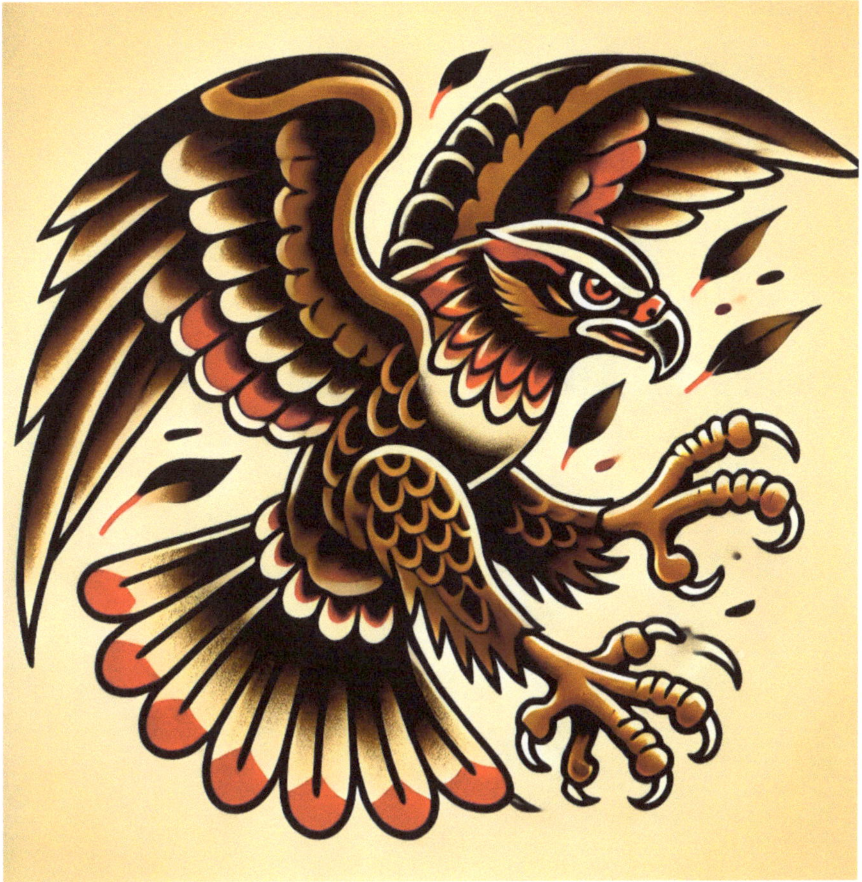

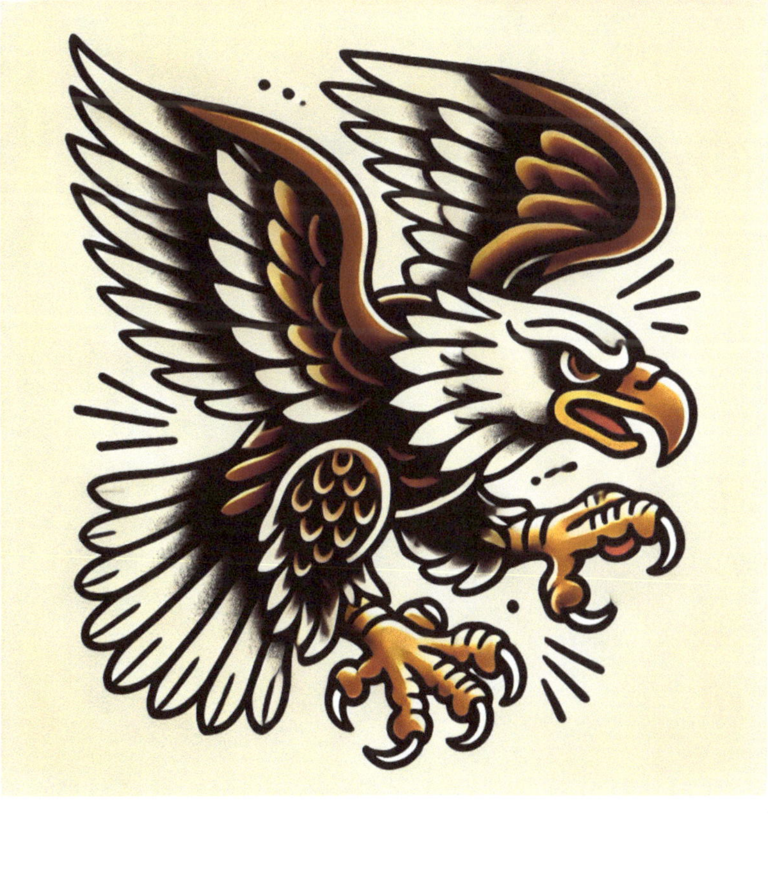

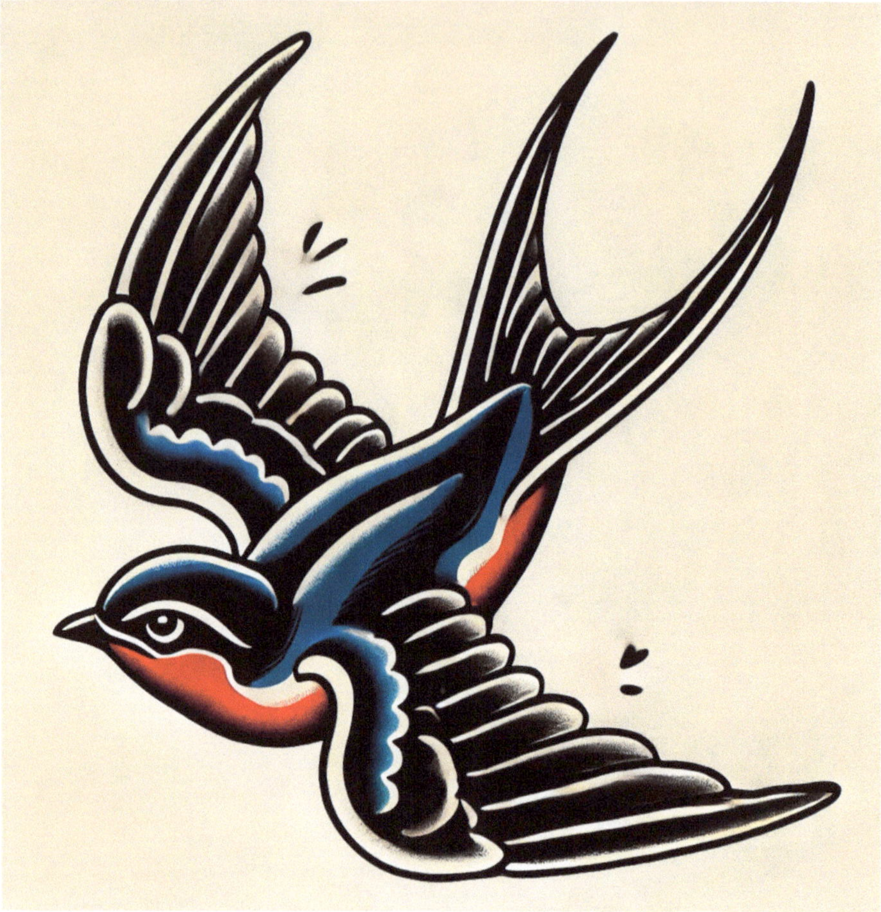

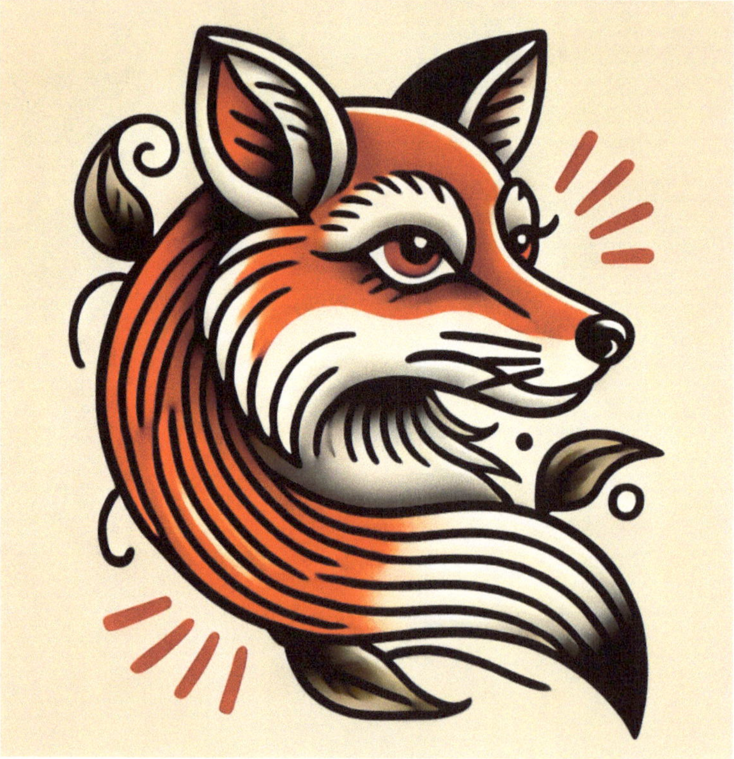

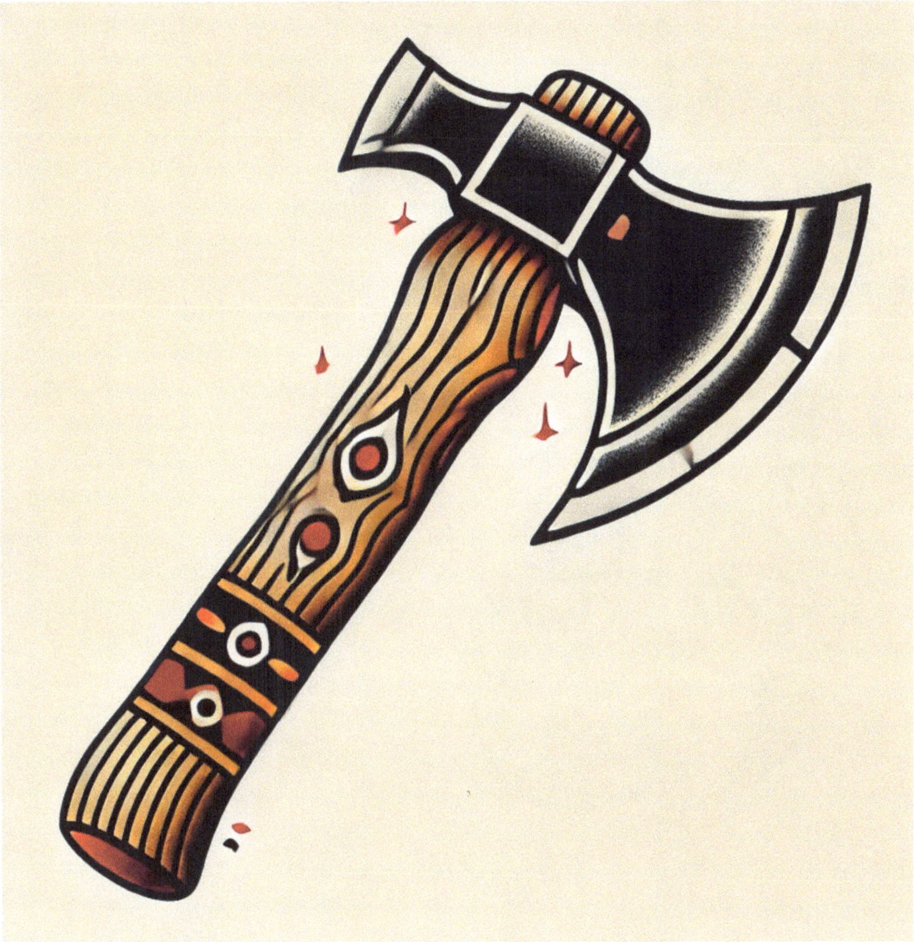

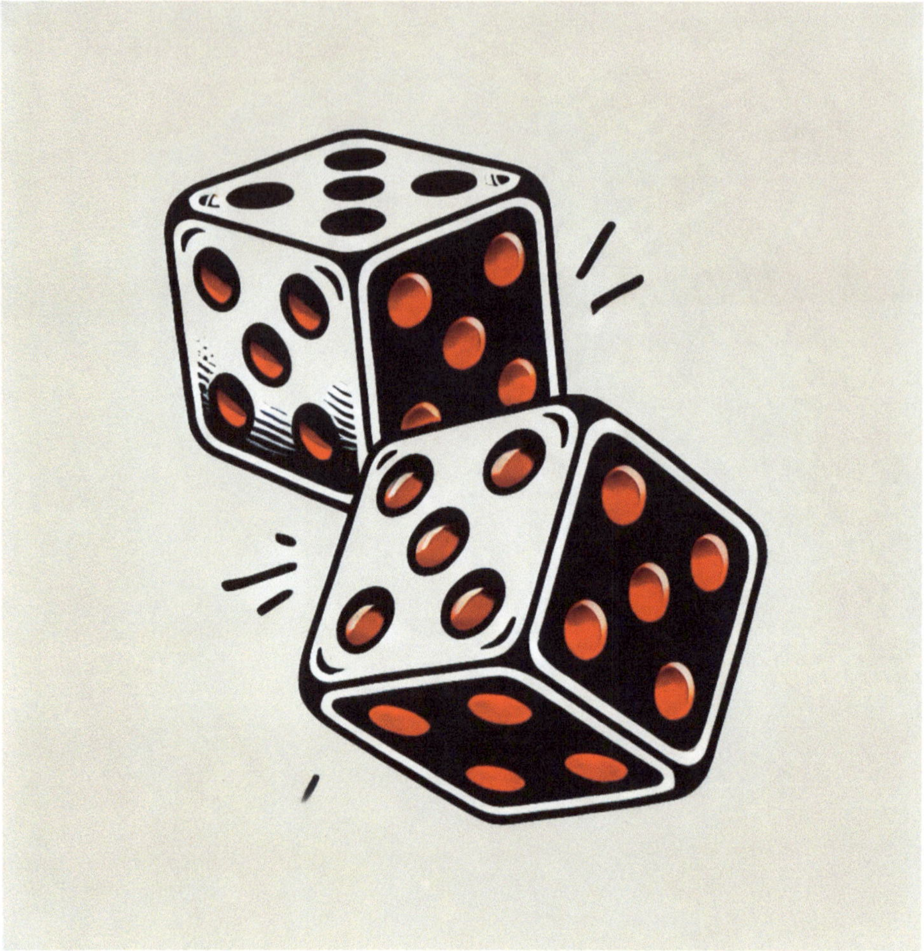

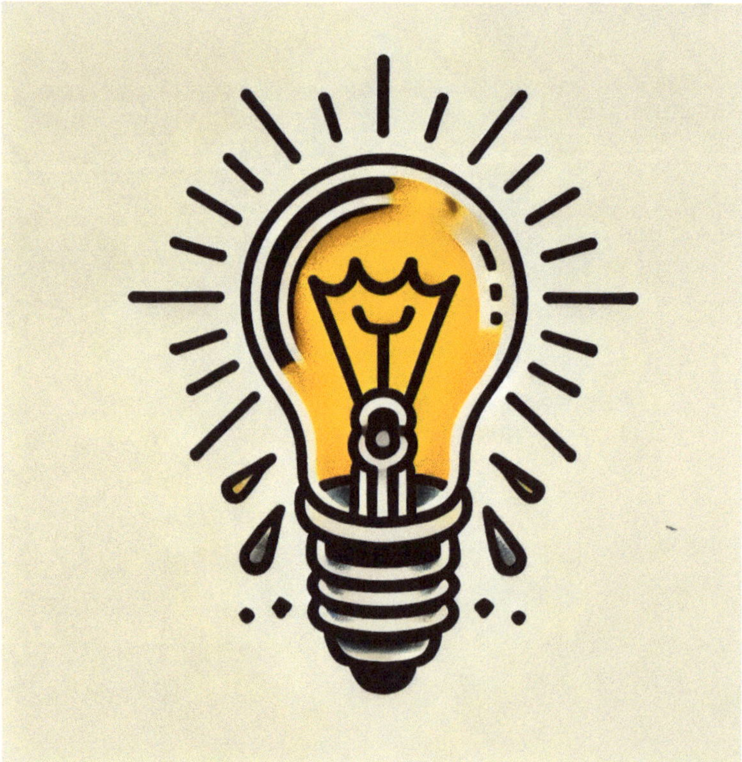

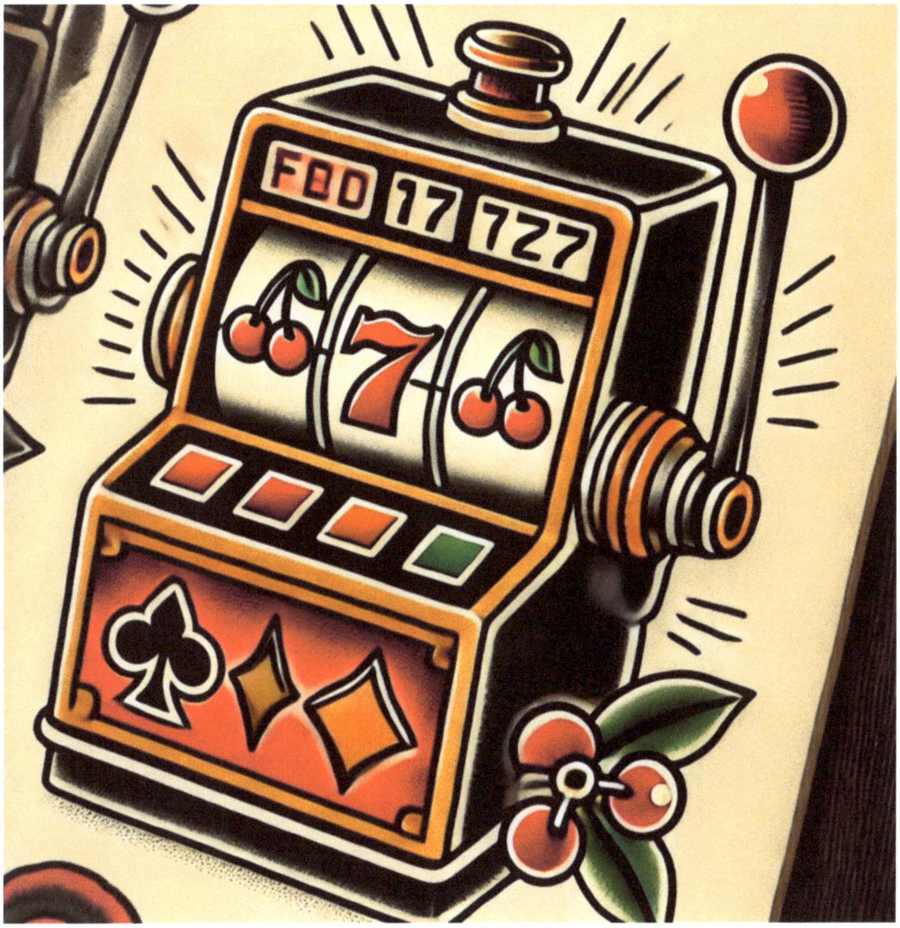
17
727

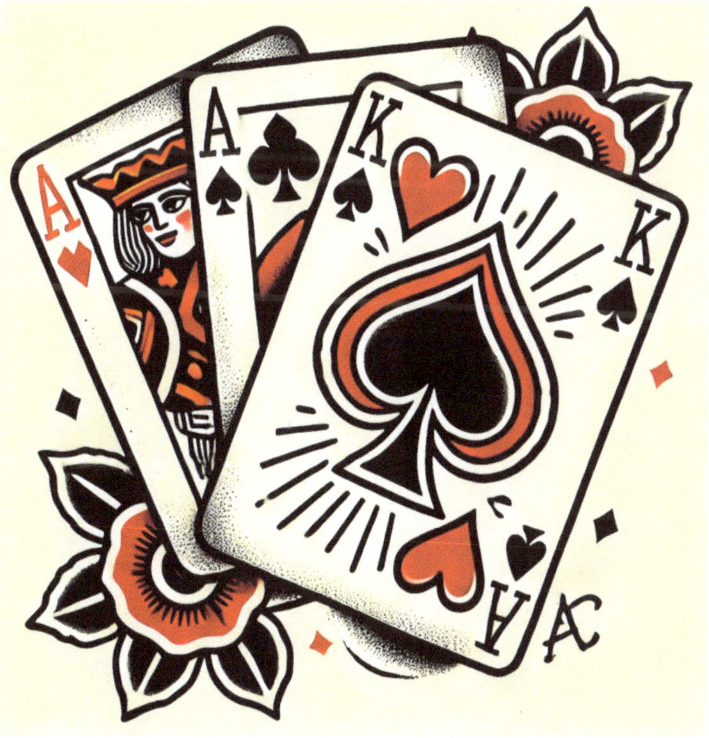

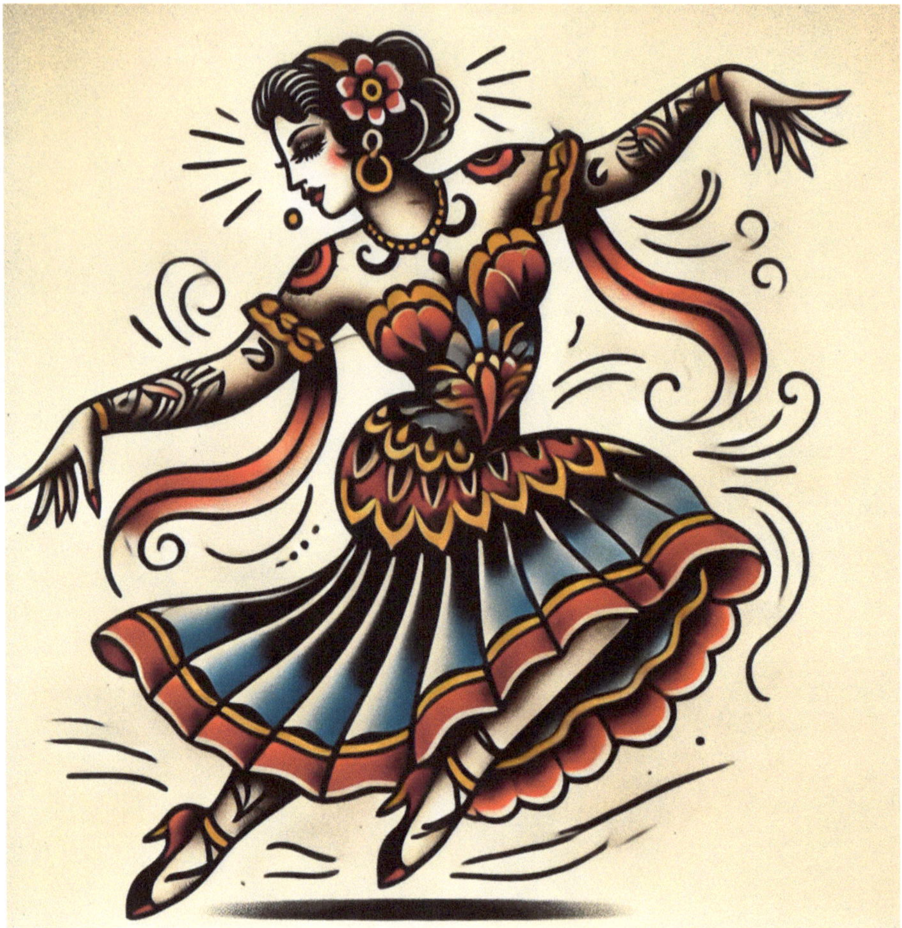

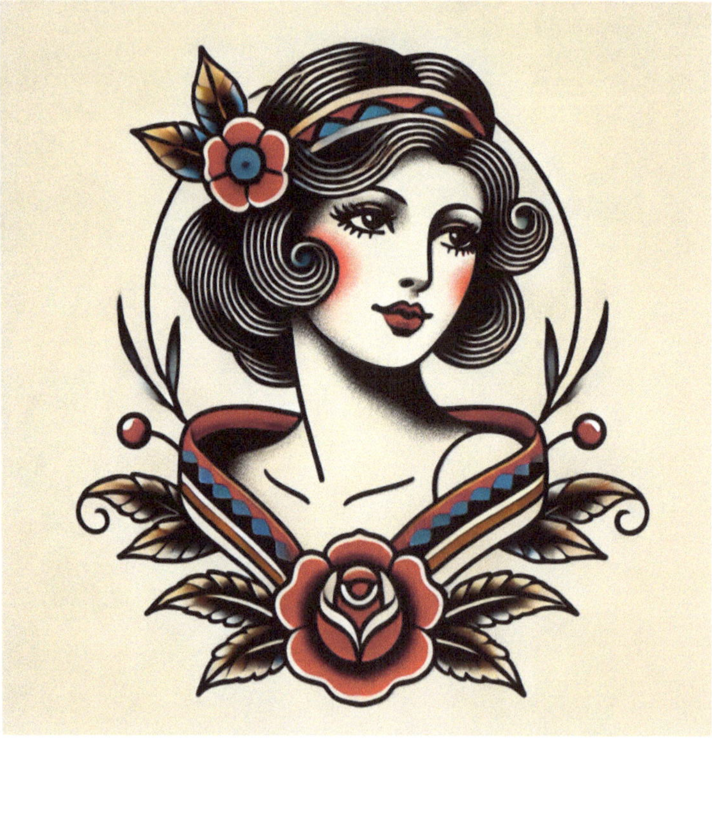

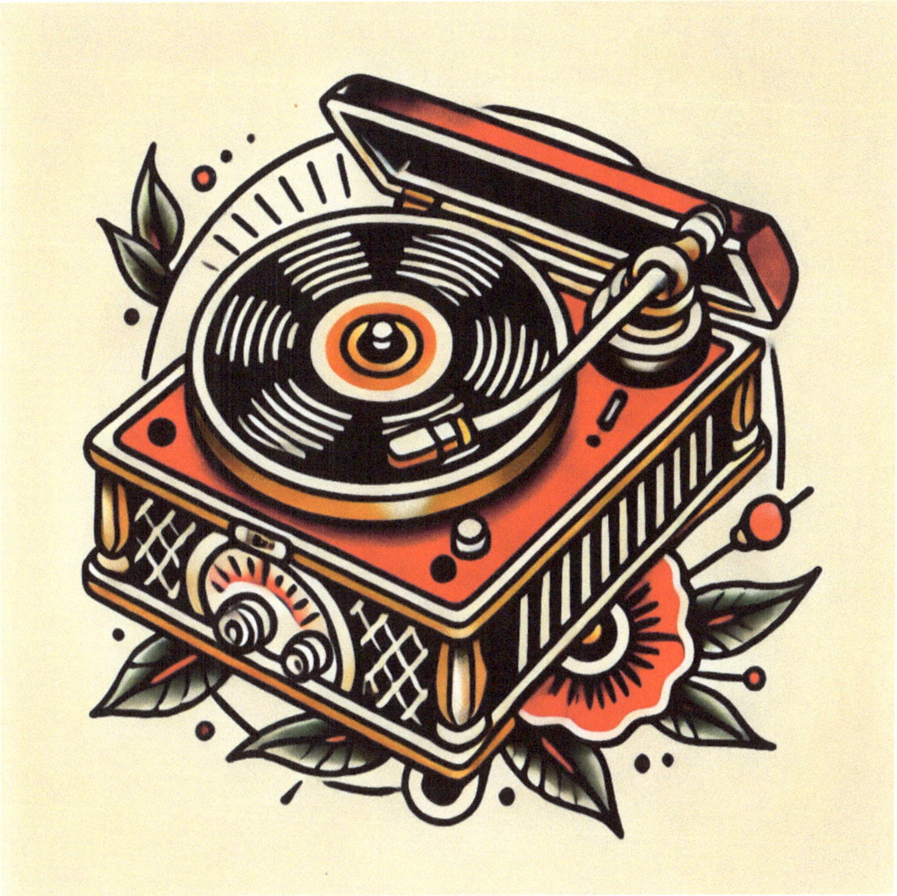

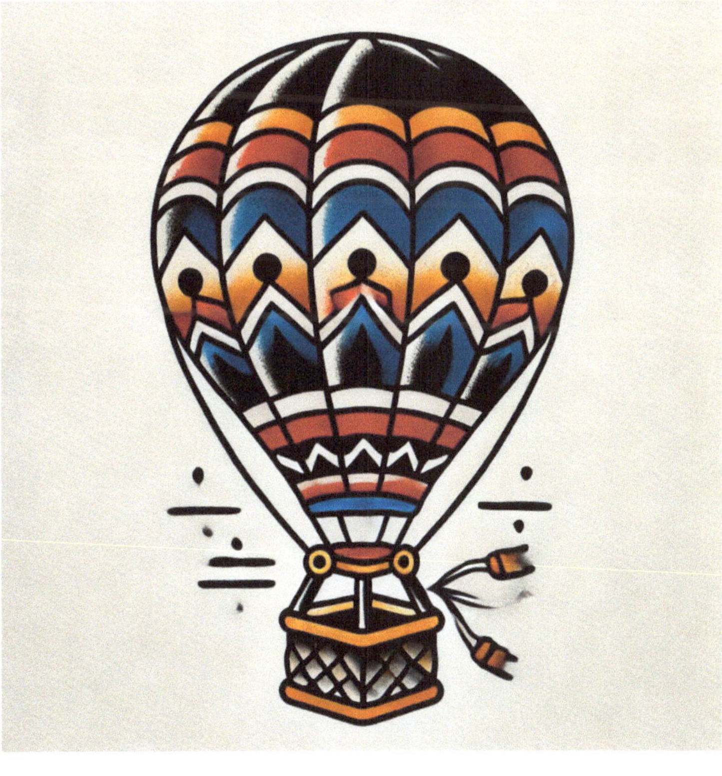

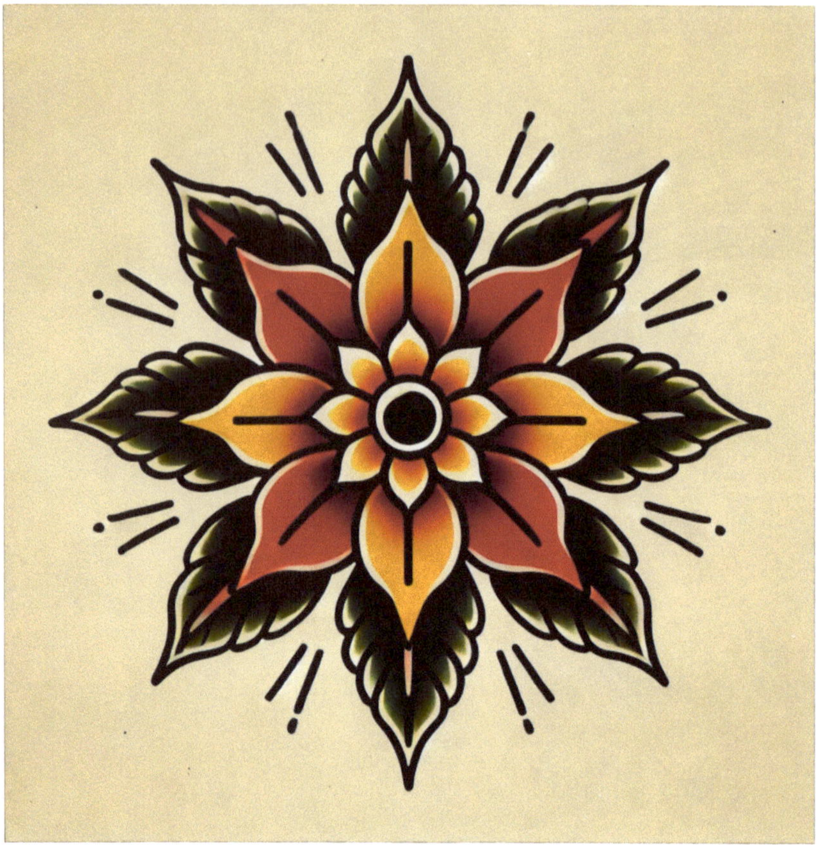

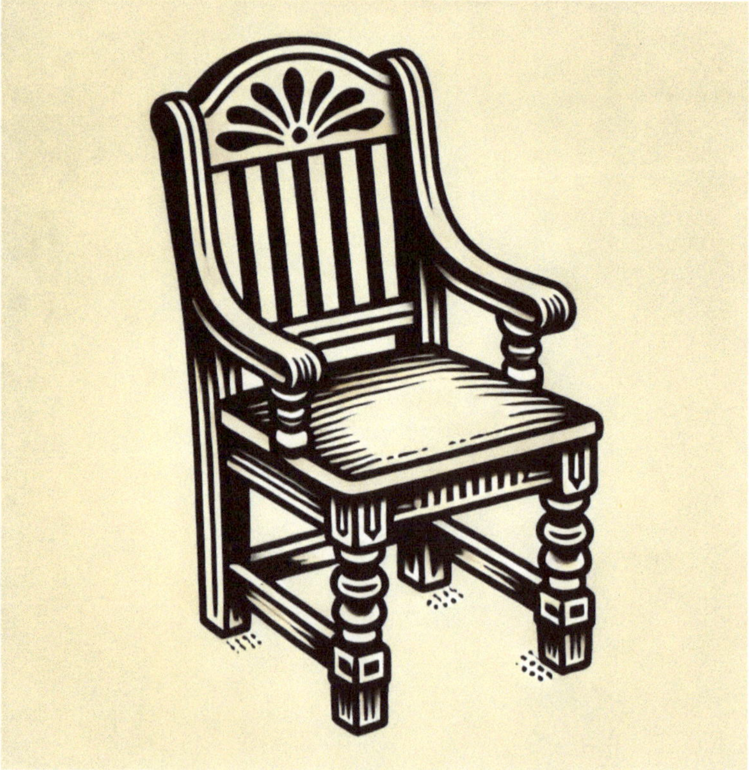

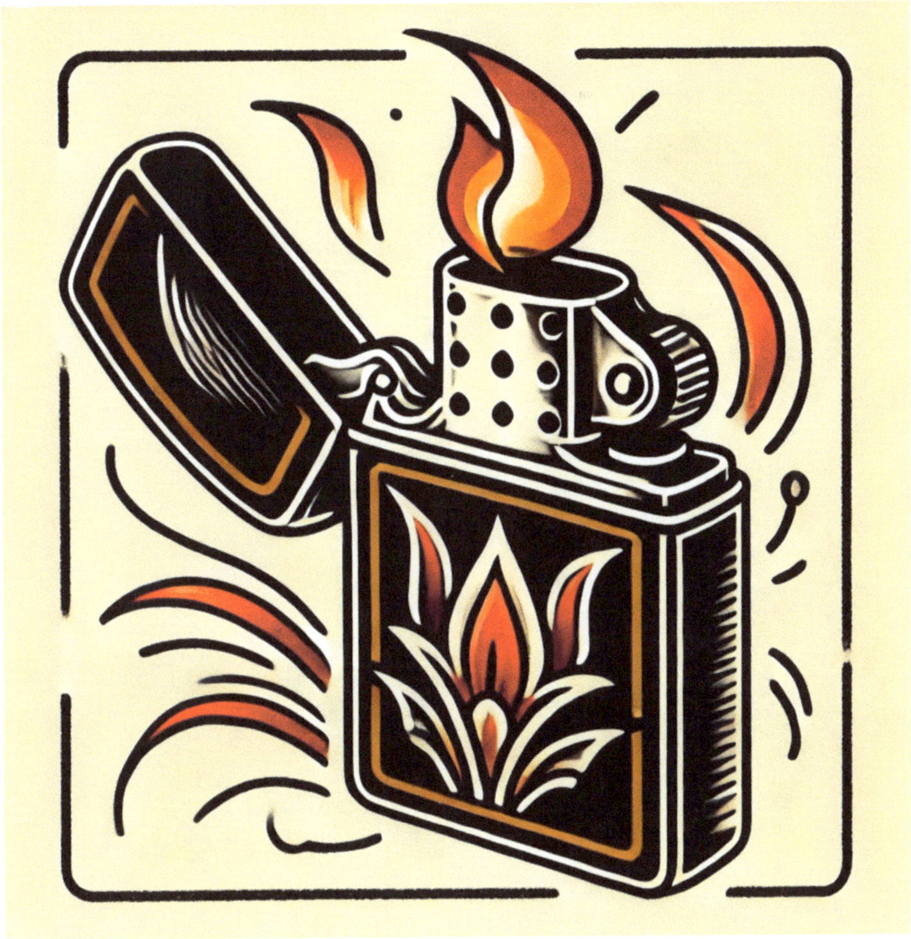

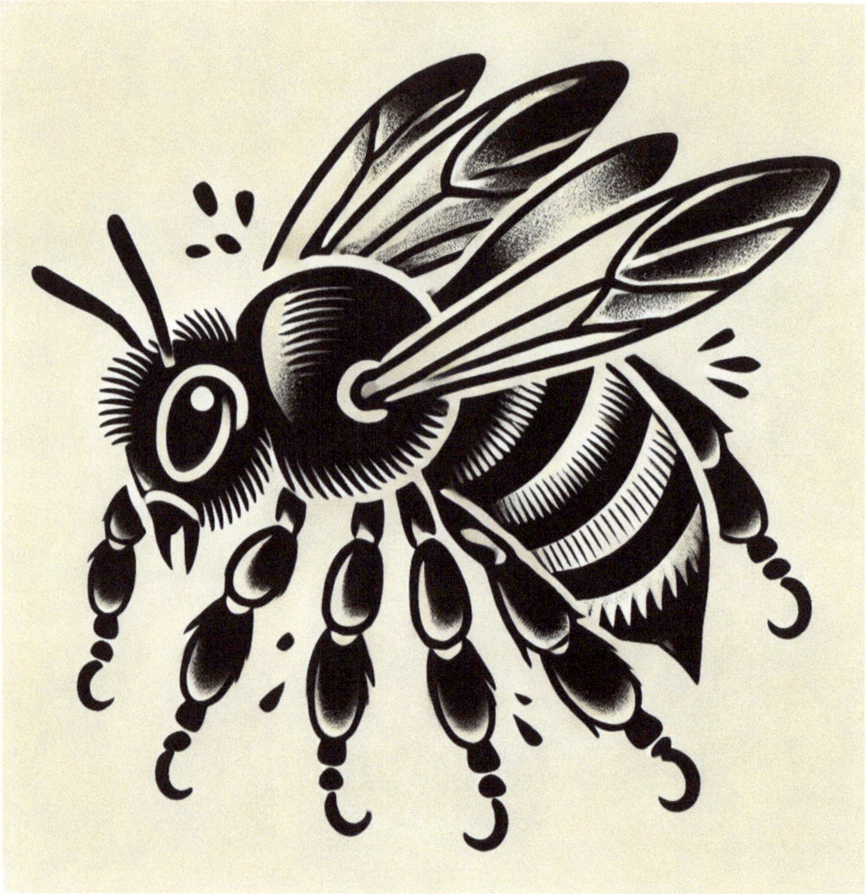

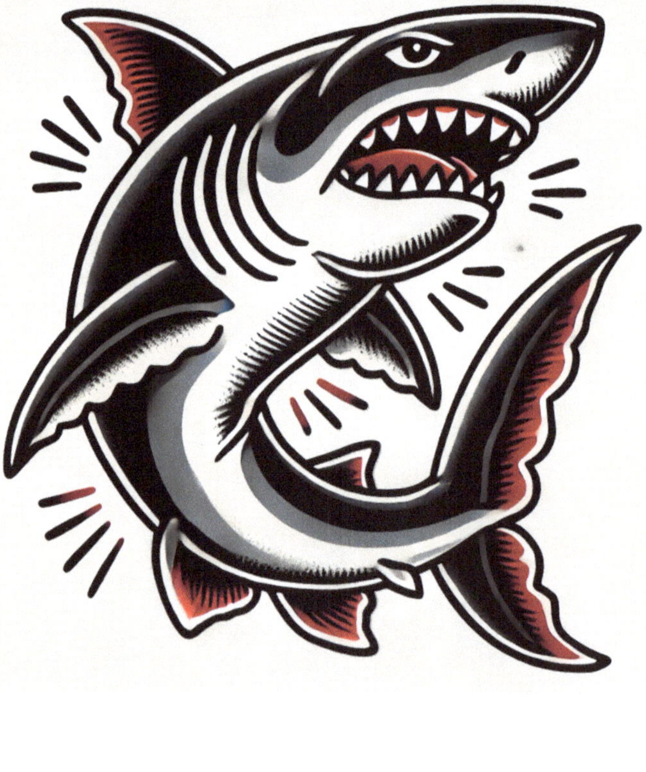

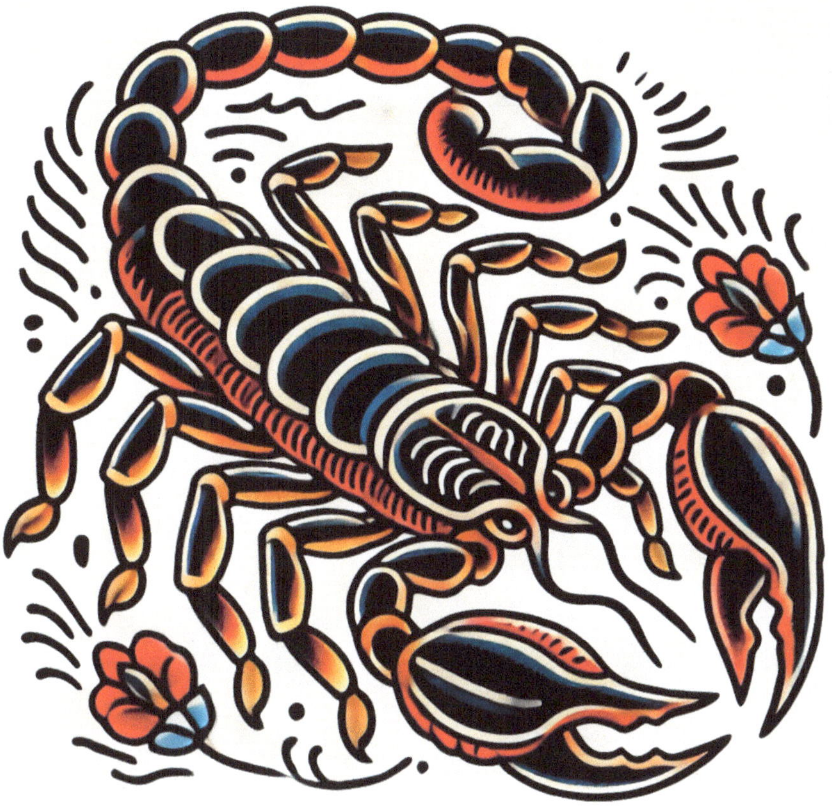

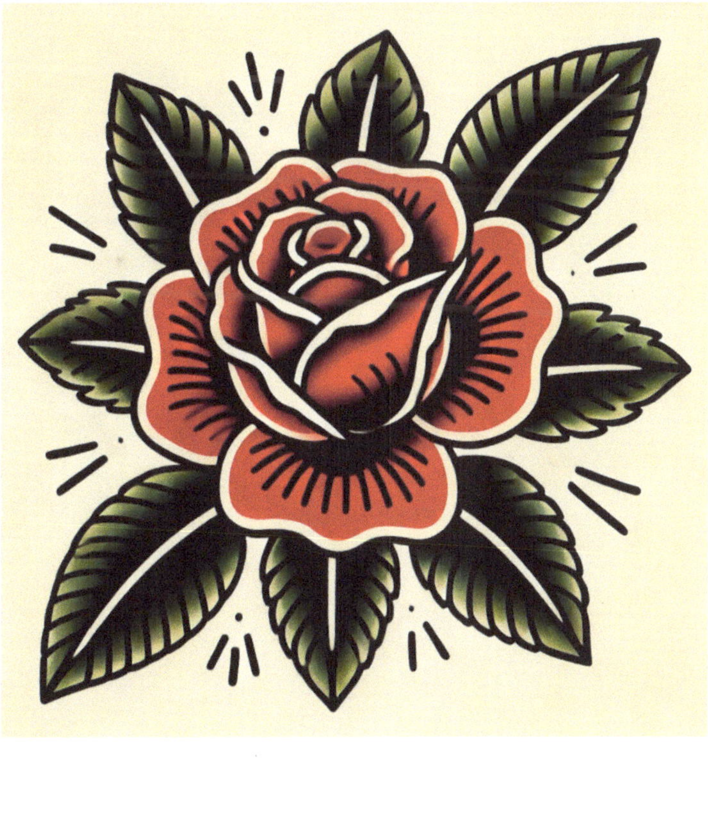

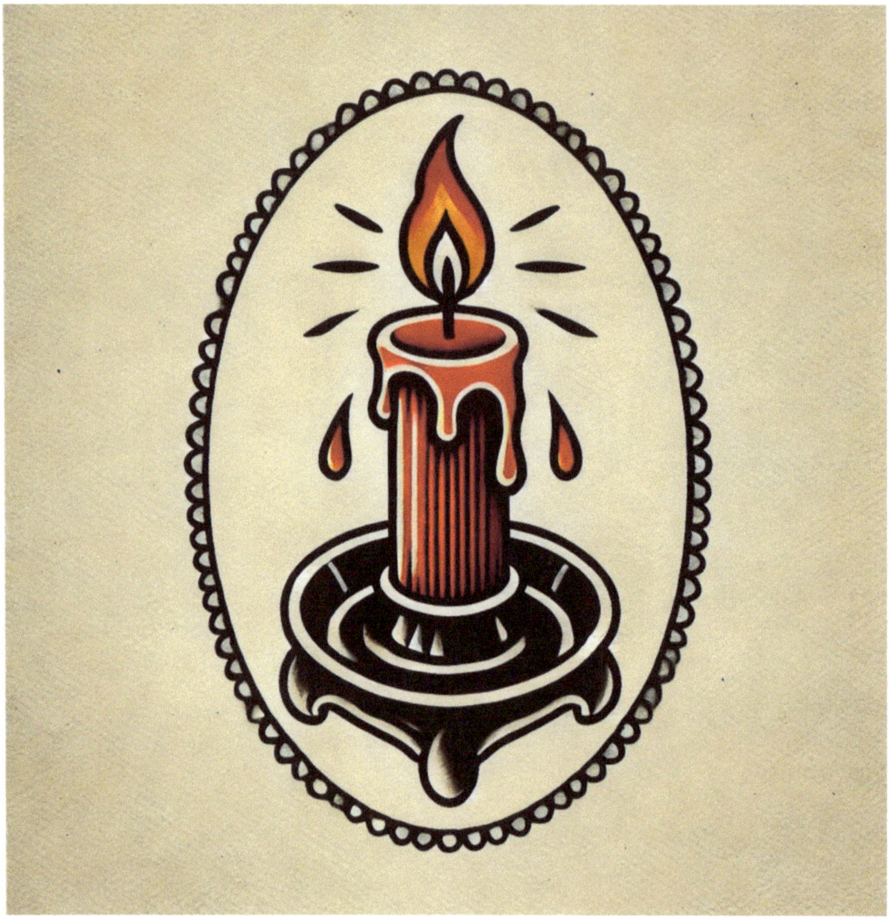

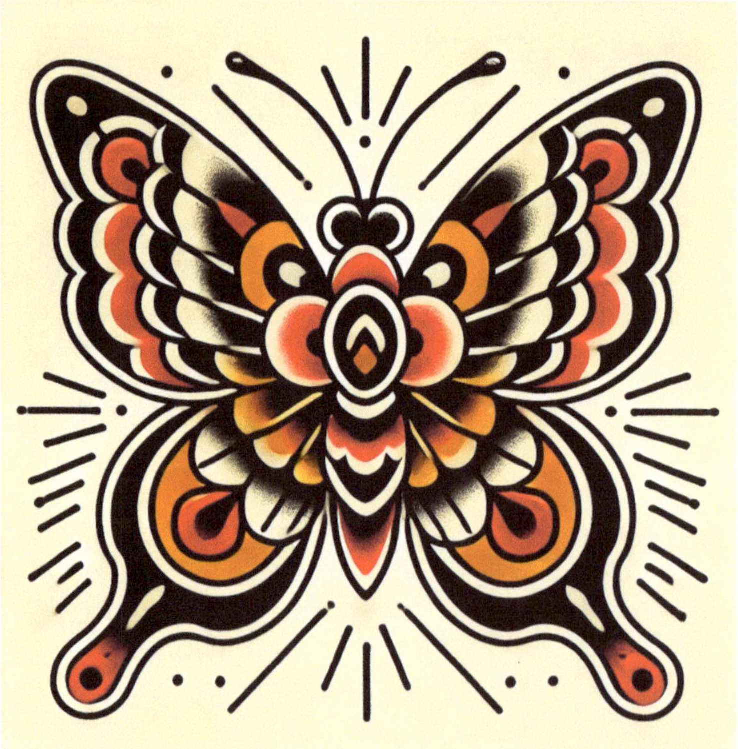

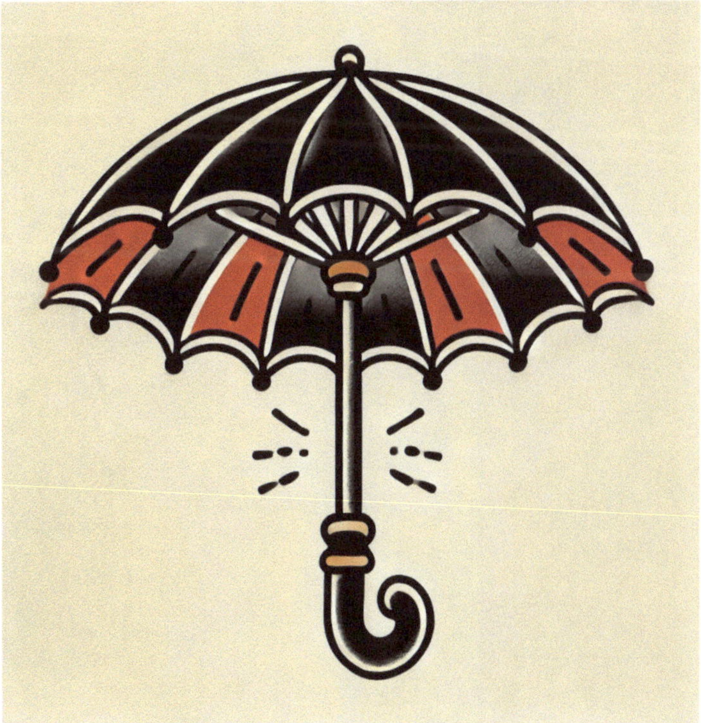

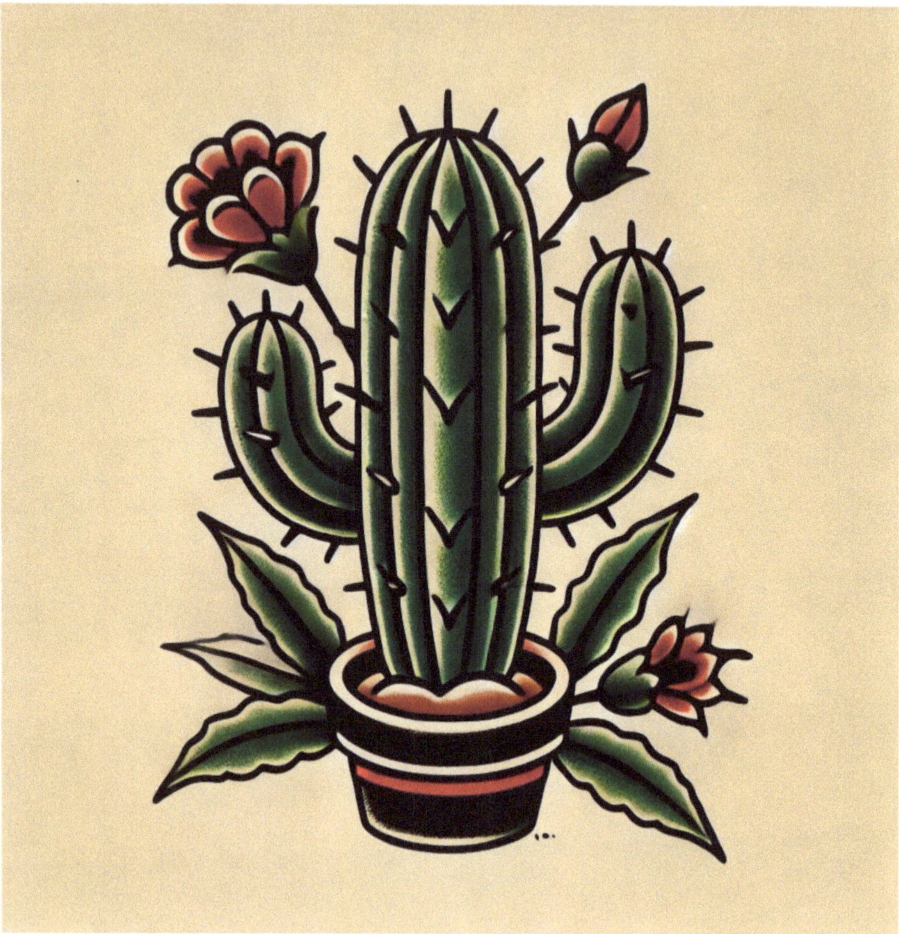

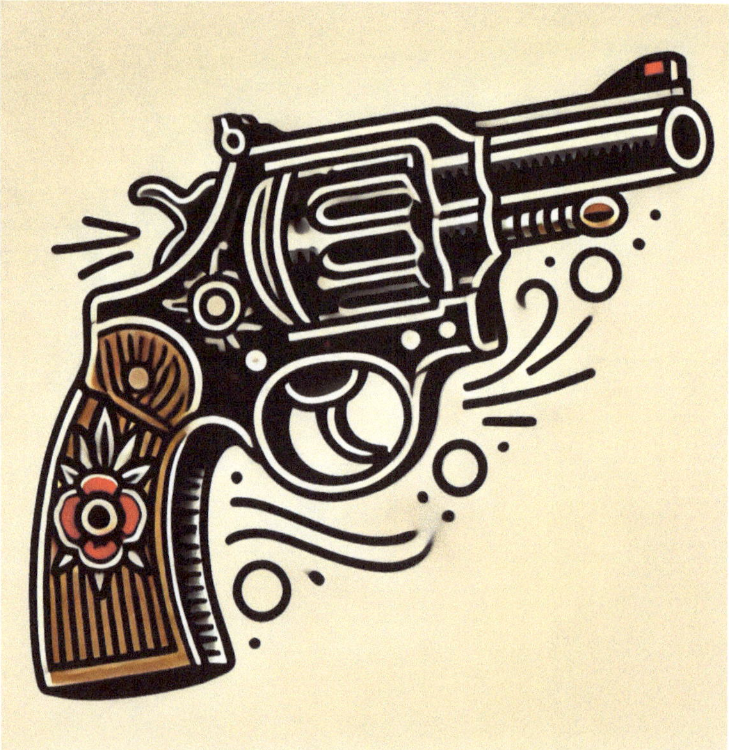

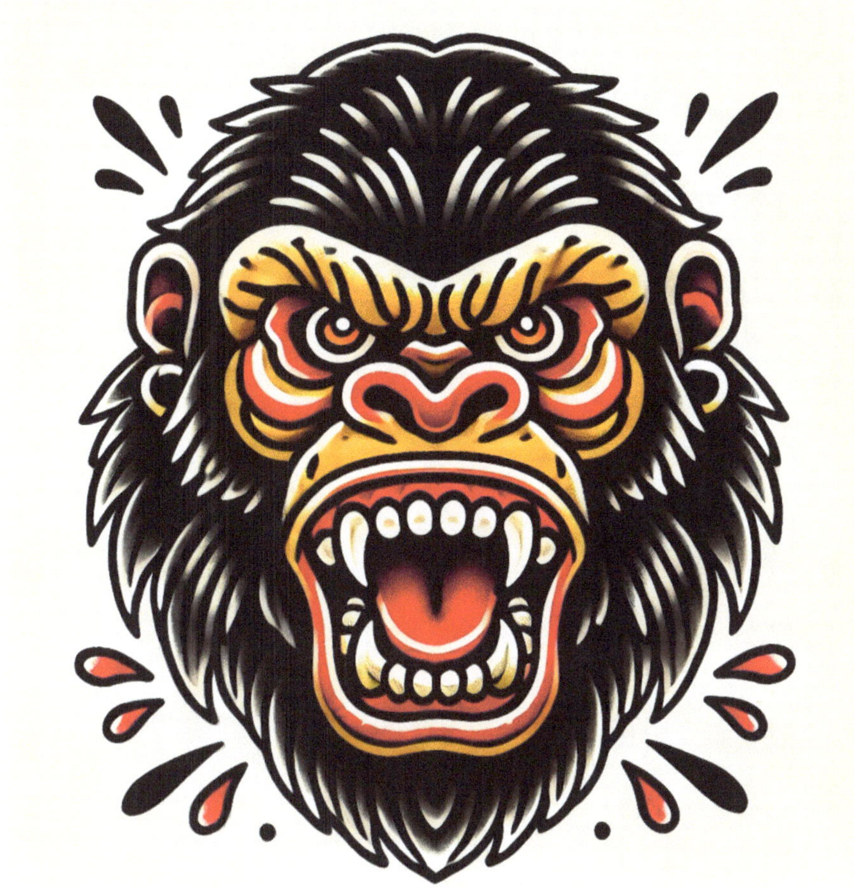

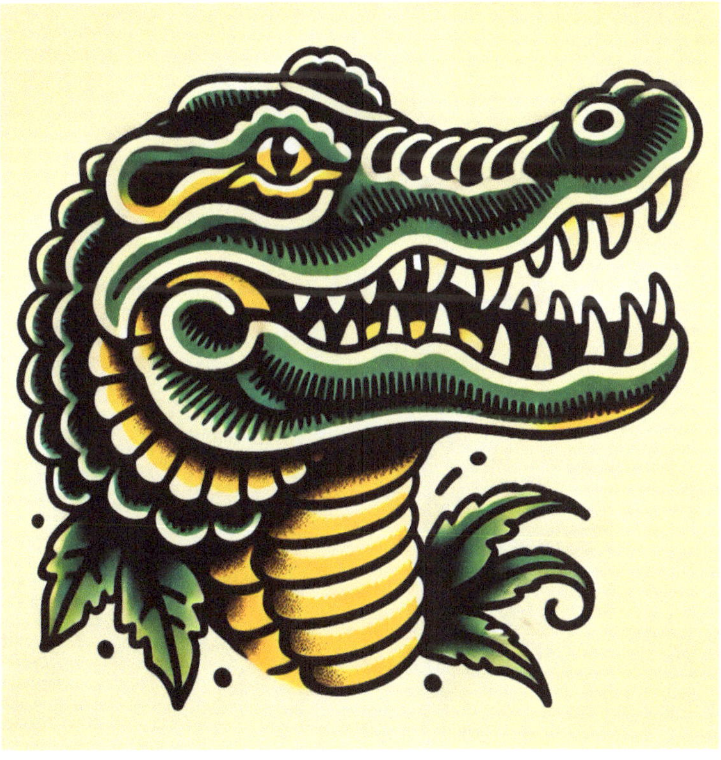

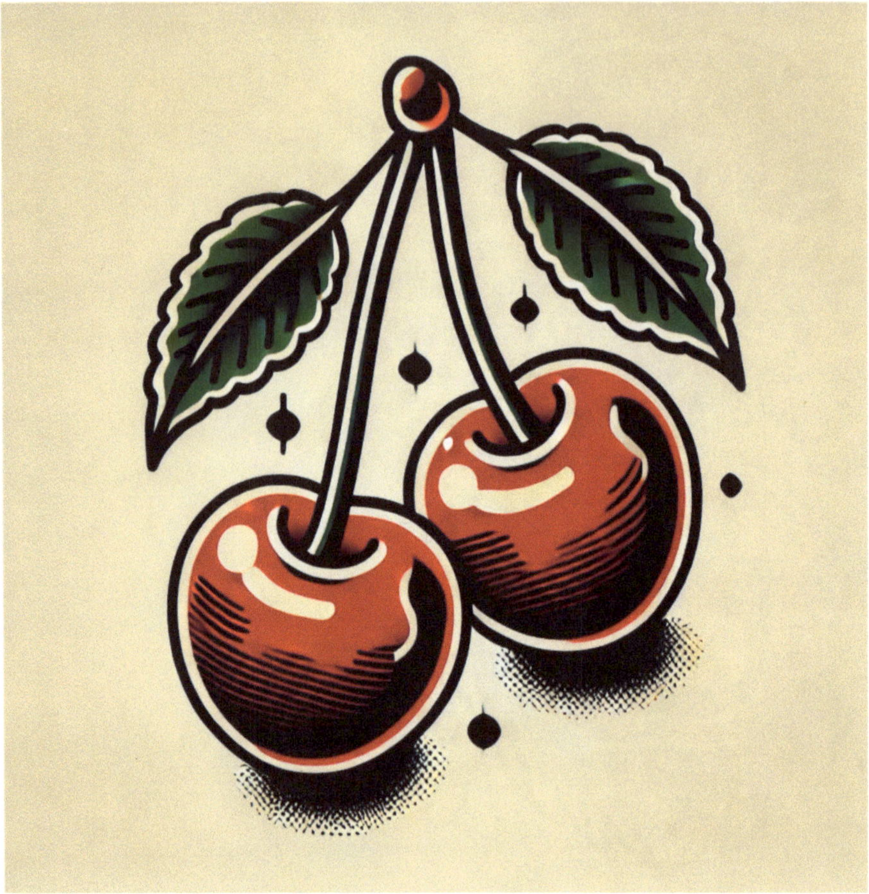

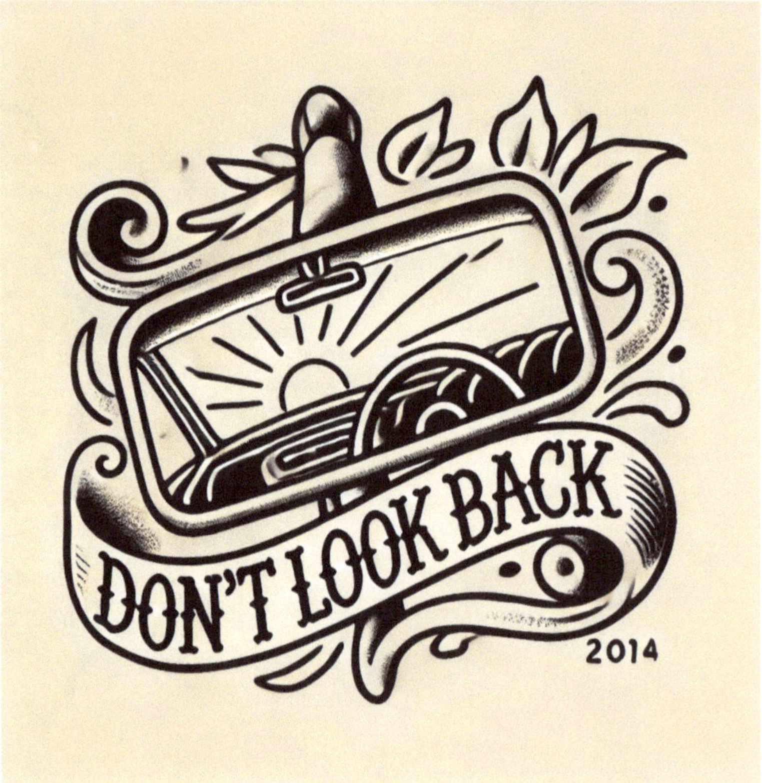
DON'T LOOK BACK
2014

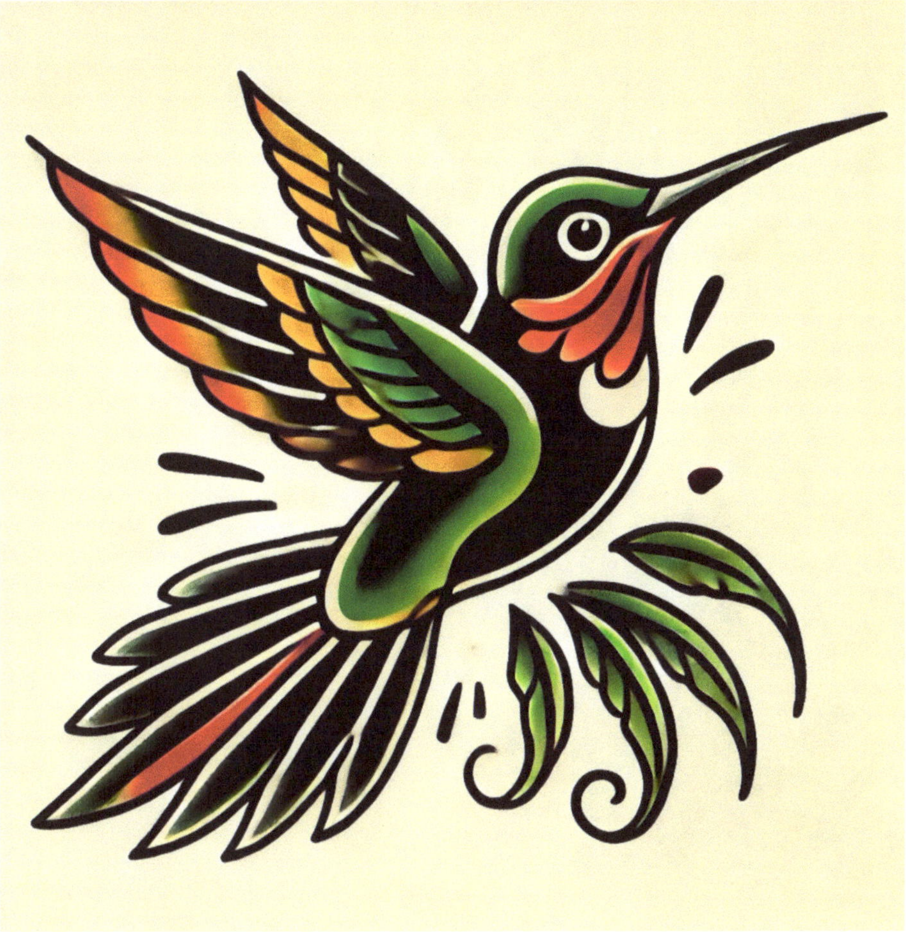

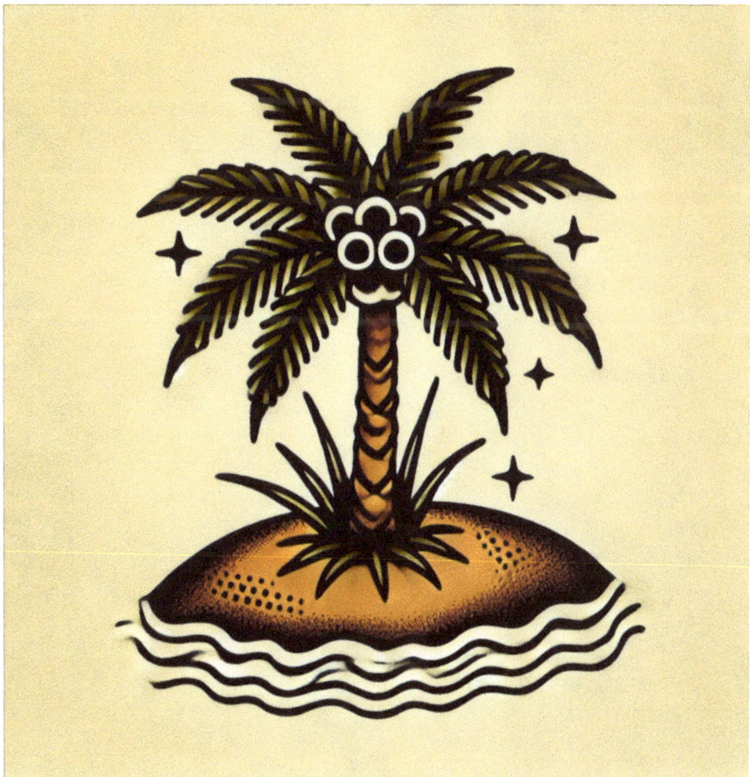

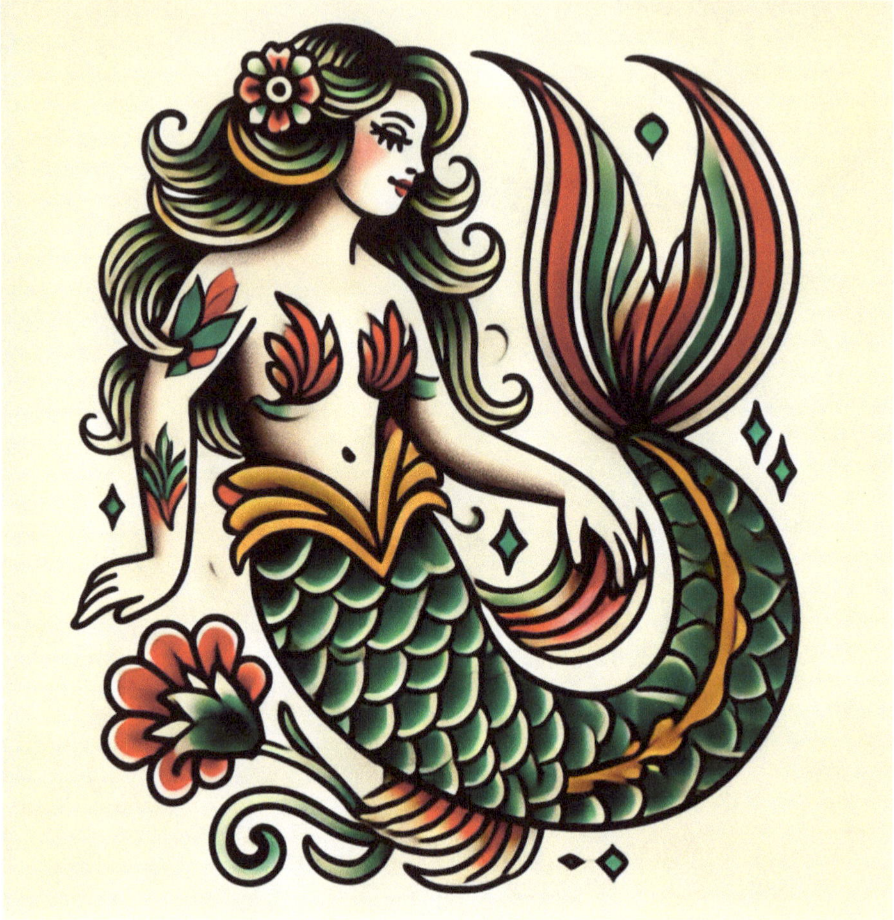

TRUE LOVE

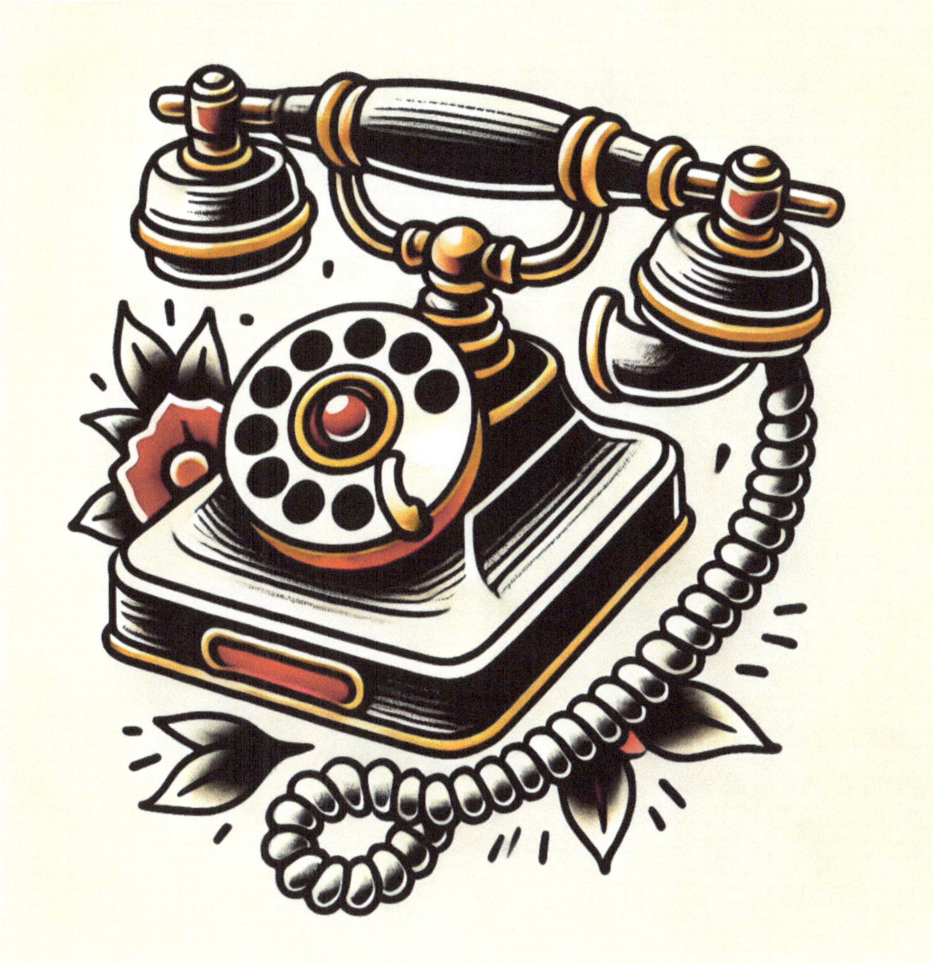

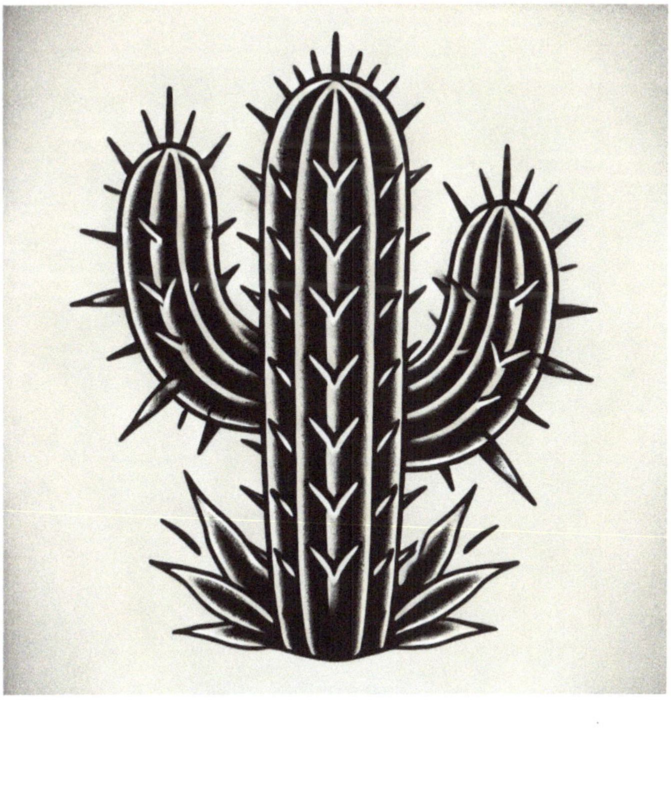

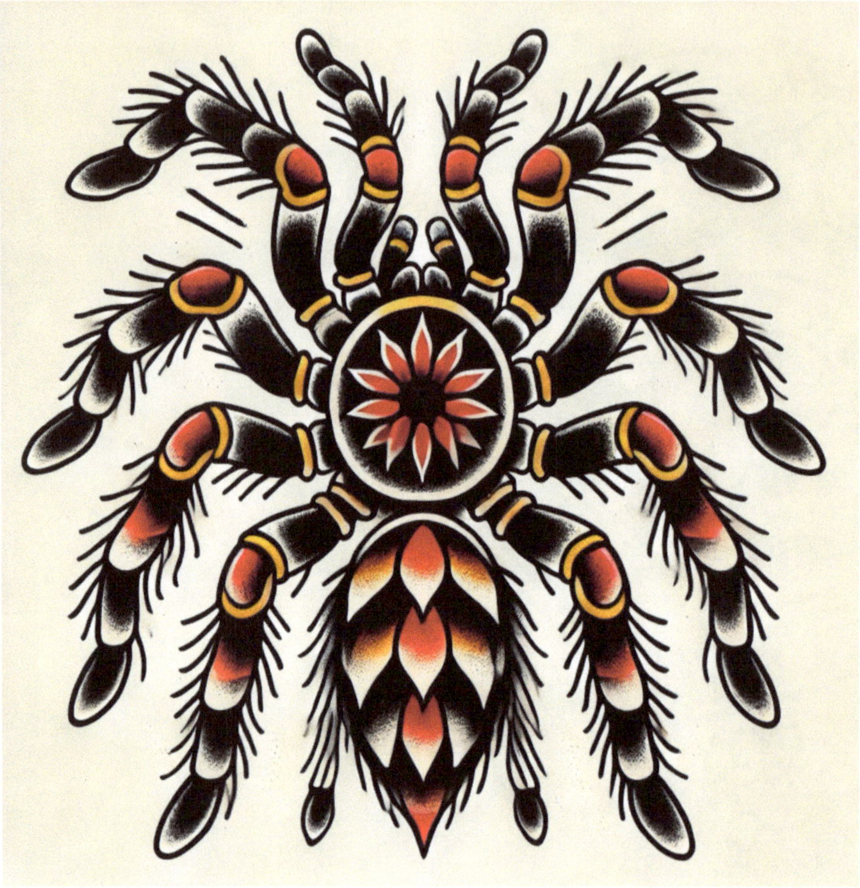

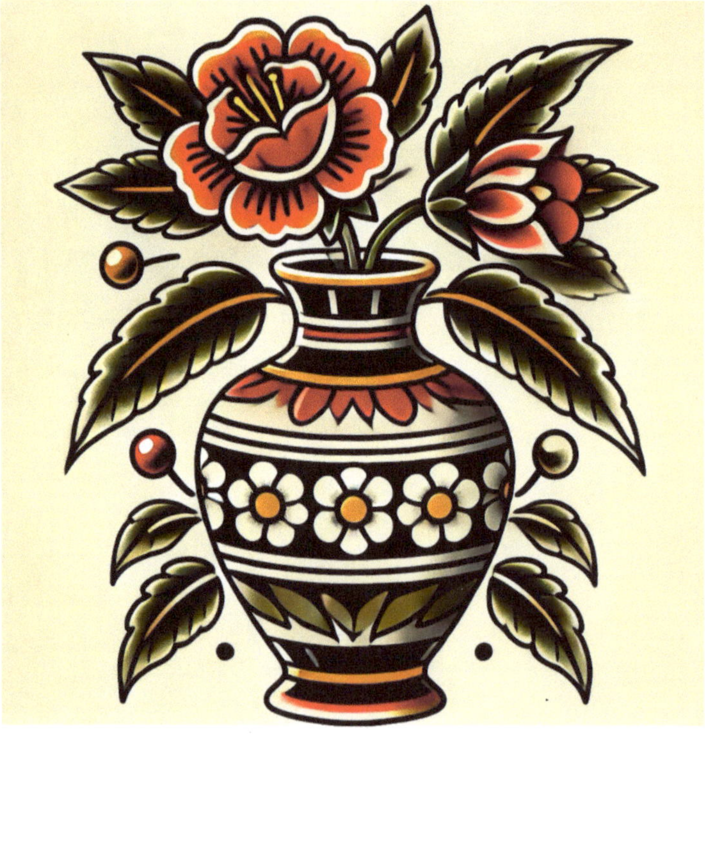

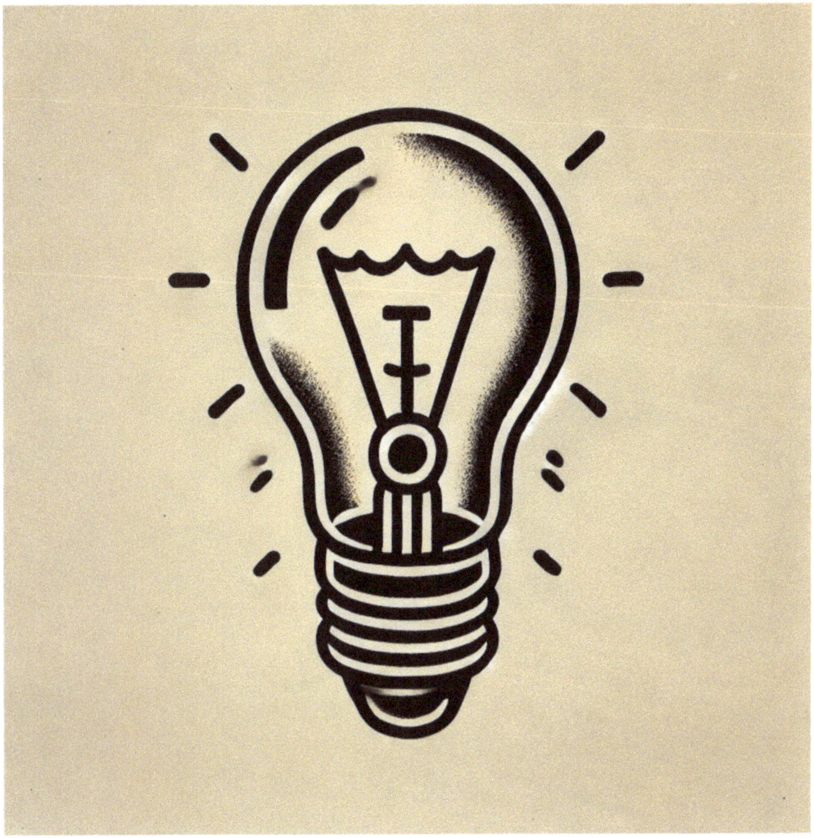

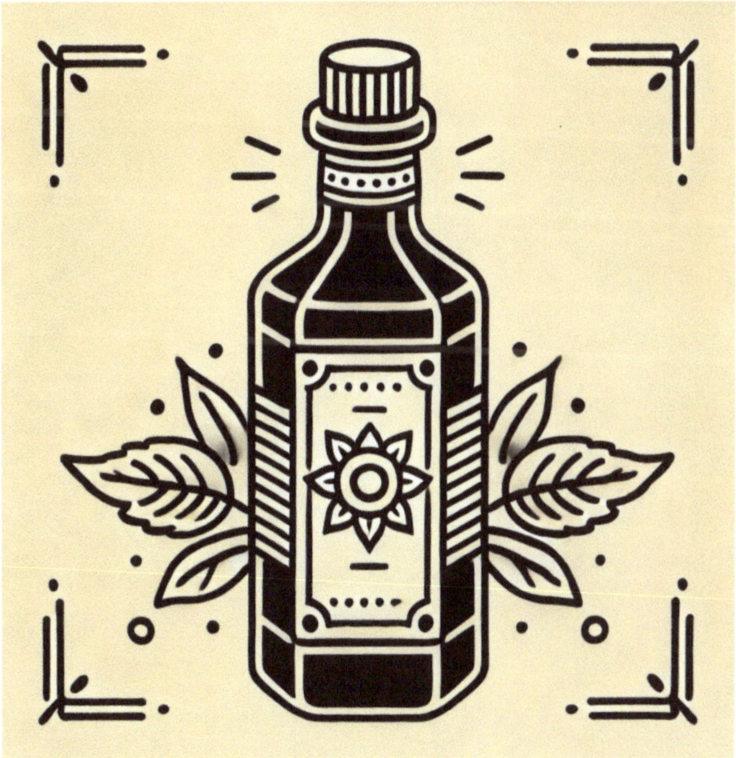

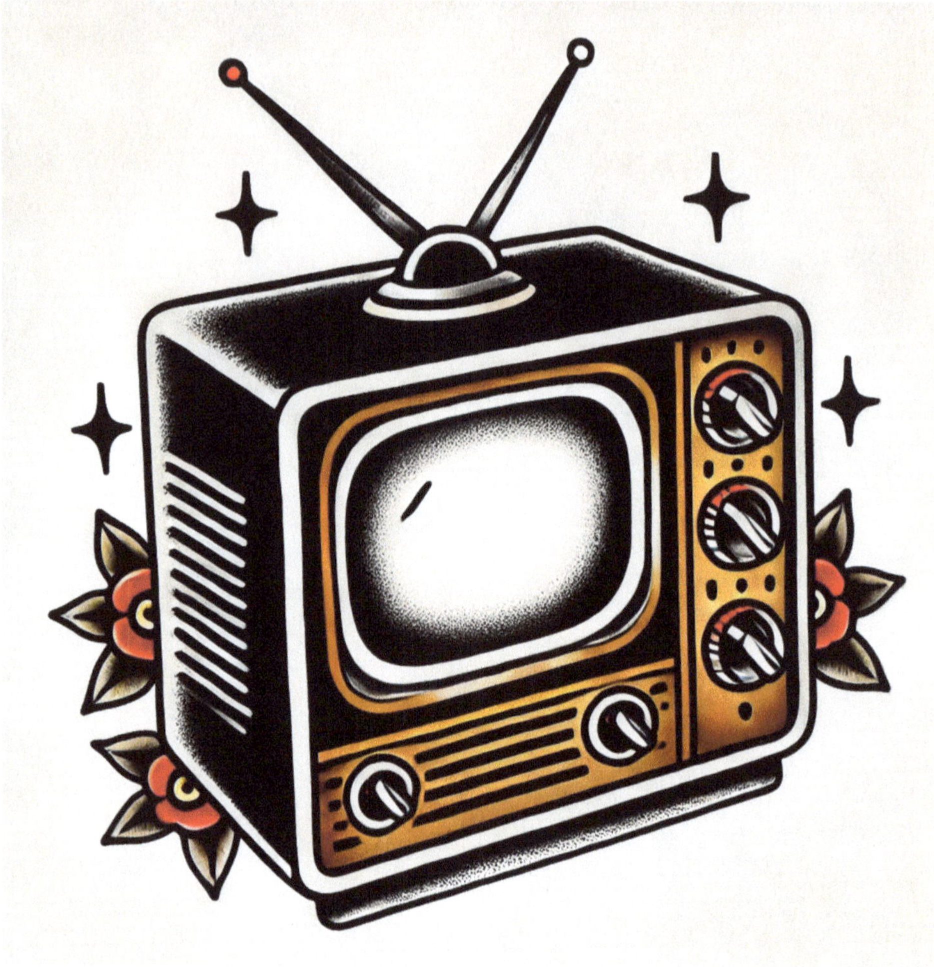

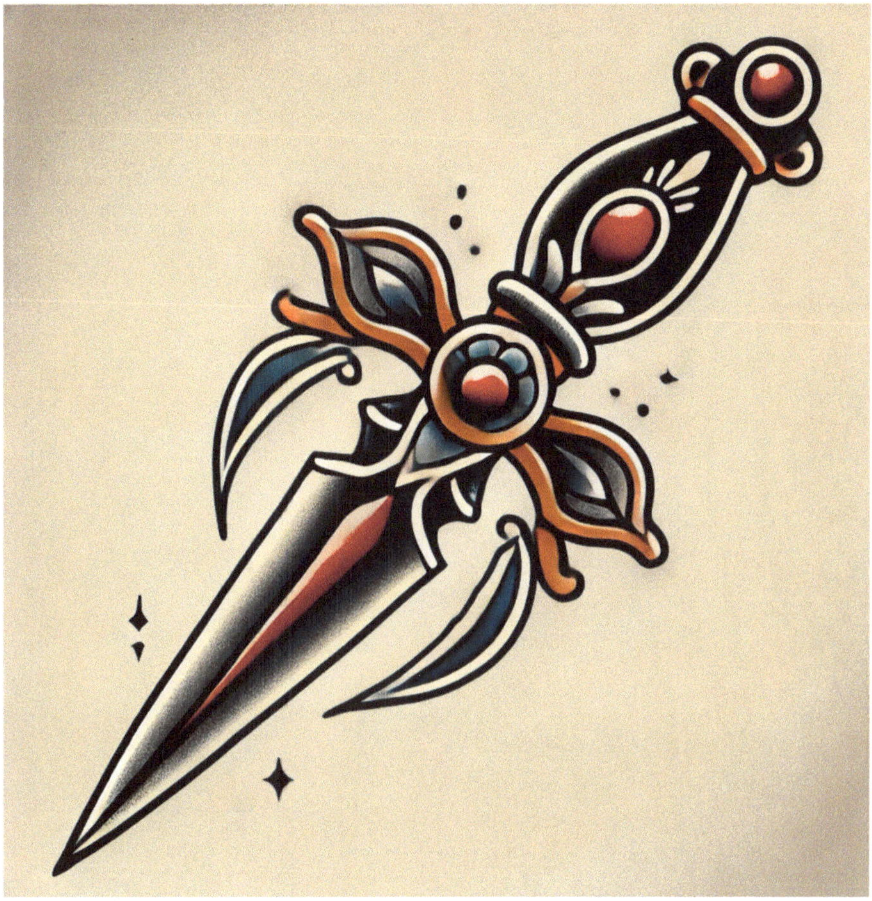

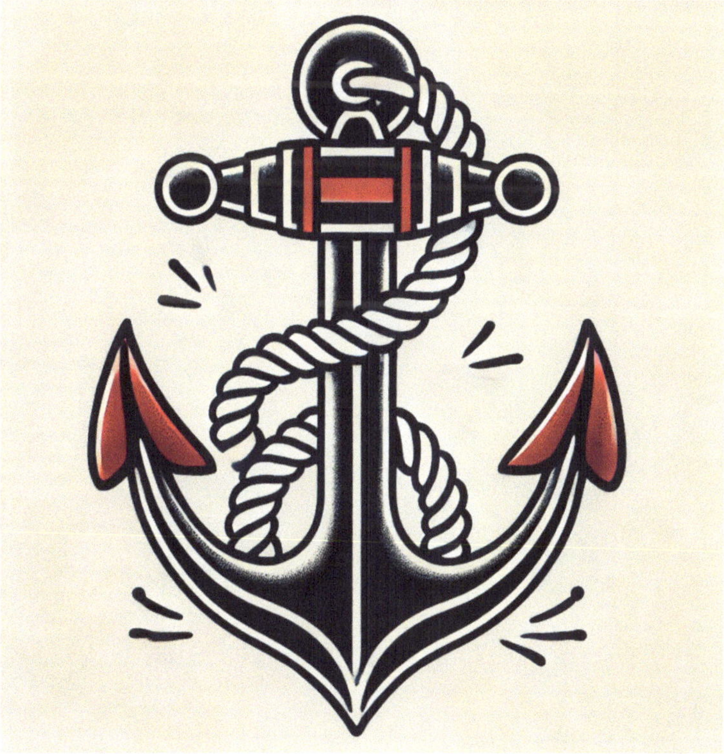

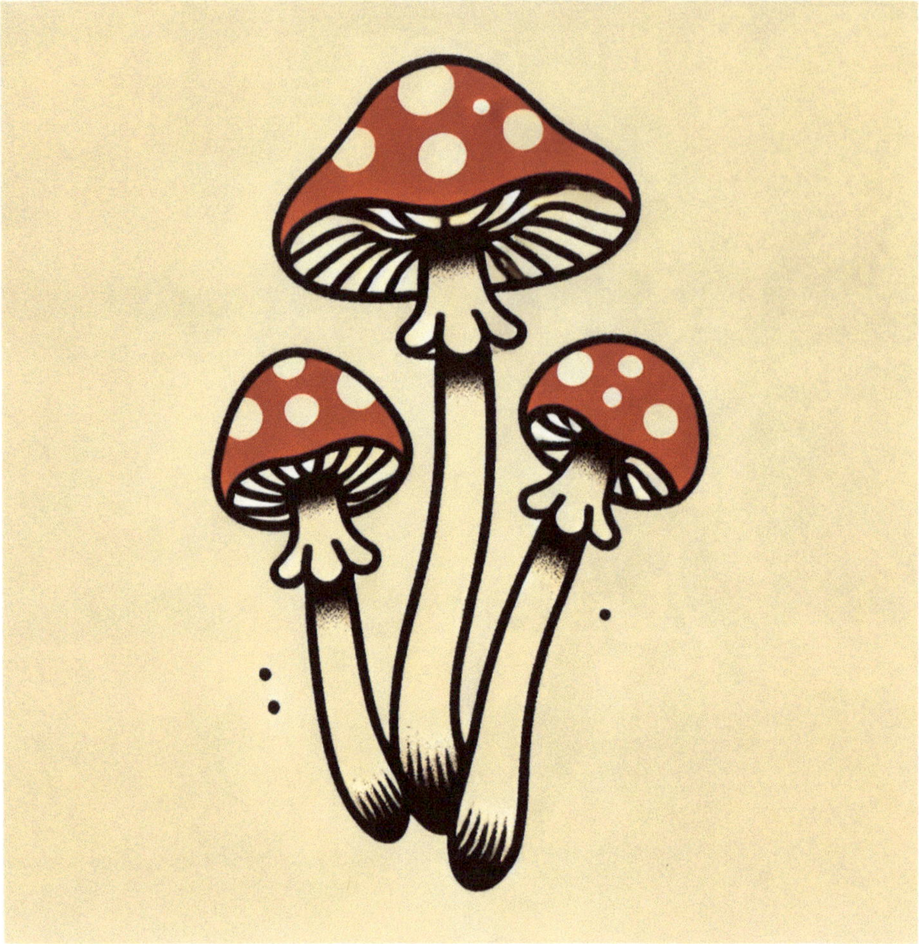

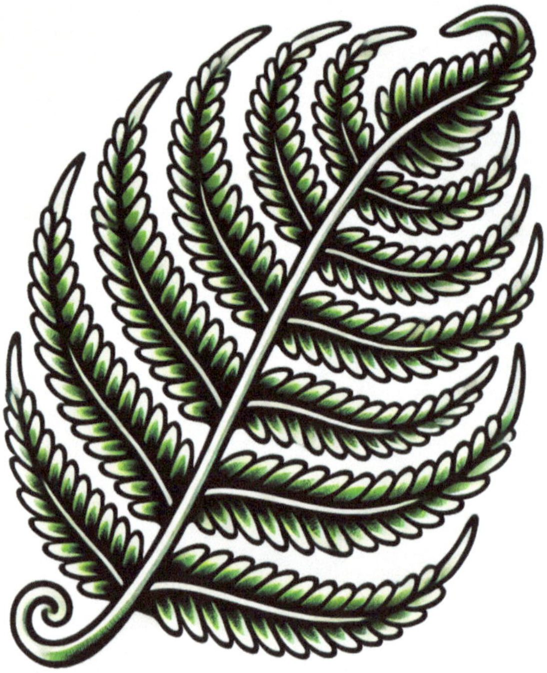

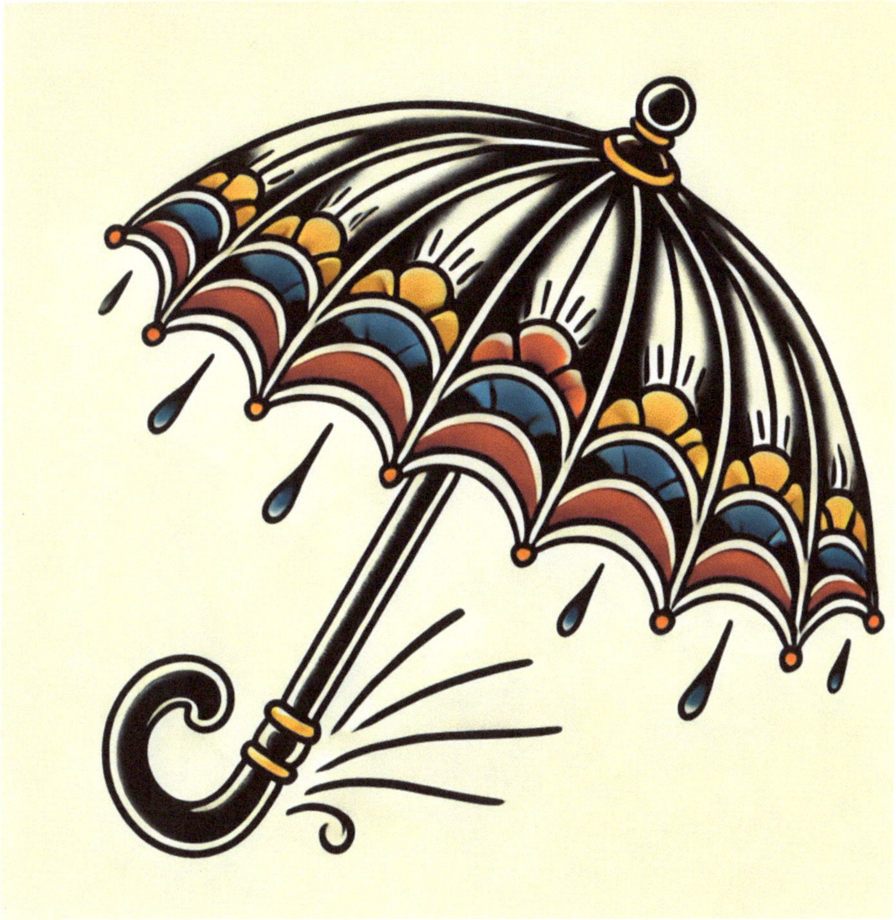

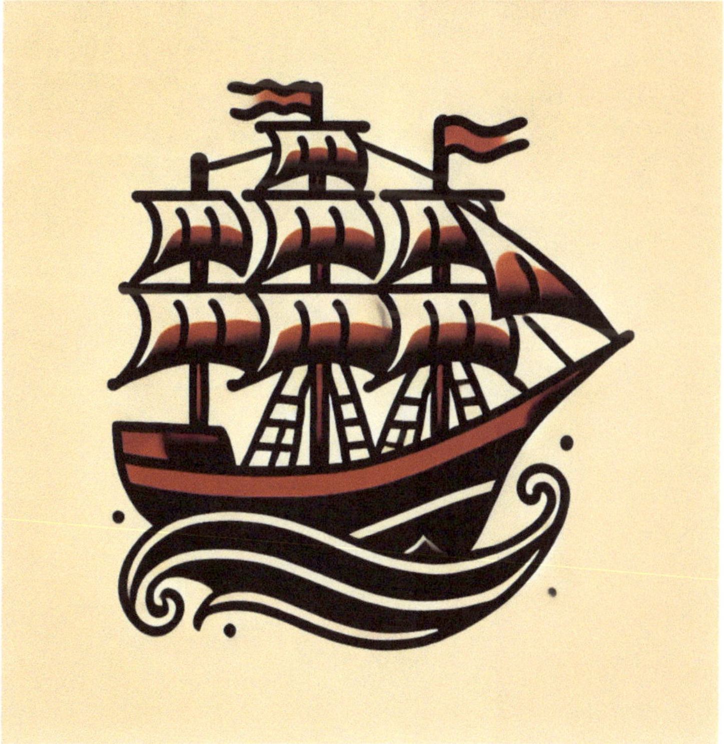

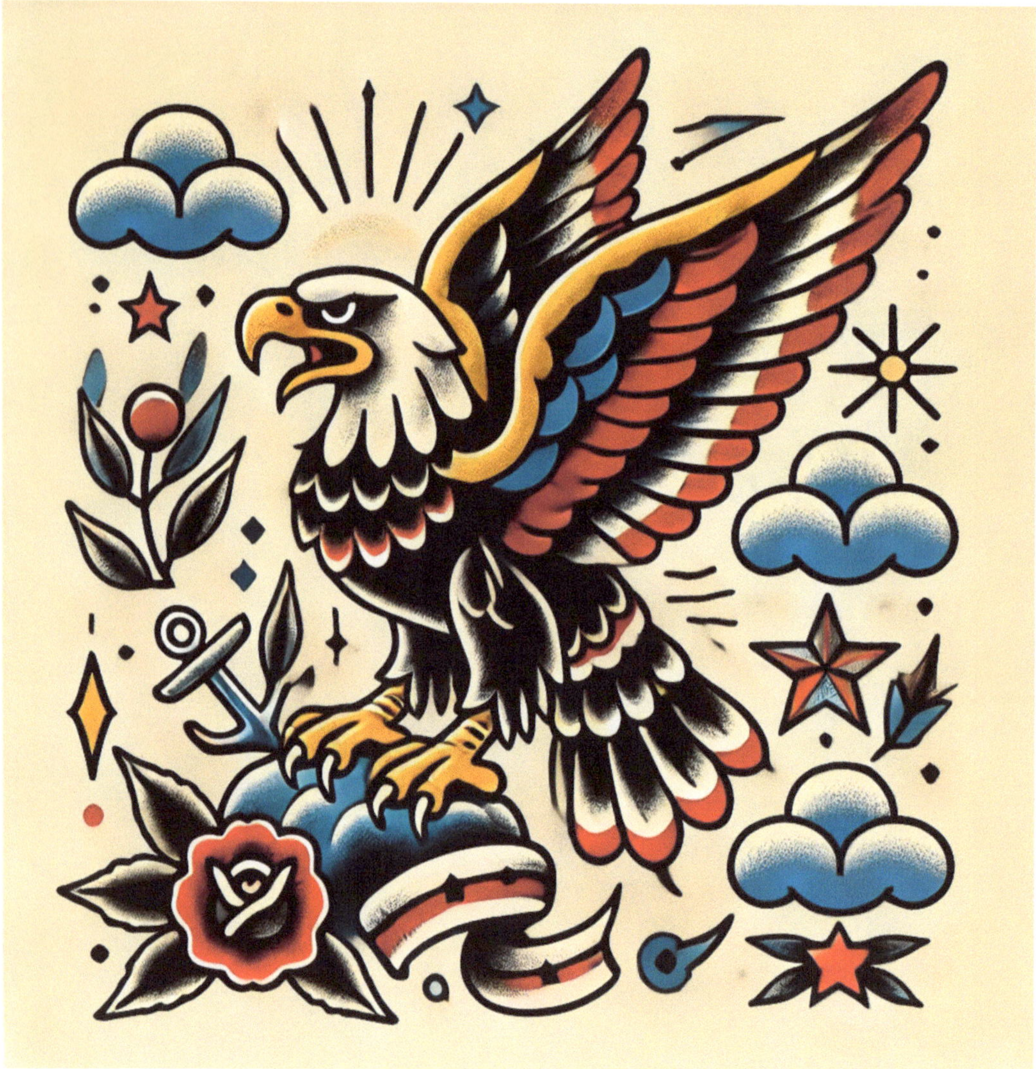

www.ingramcontent.com/pod-product-compliance
Lightning Source LLC
Chambersburg PA
CBHW051820210526
45473CB00005B/1673
* 9 7 9 8 3 0 3 5 3 6 6 7 8 *